PAGAN SIGILS
Illustrated Guide to the Non Christian
Symbols of Western Occultism

M B JACKSON

Green Magic

Pagan Sigils © 2022 by Mark Jackson.
All rights reserved. No part of this book may be used or reproduced in any form without written permission of the author, except in the case of quotations in articles and reviews.

Green Magic
53 Brooks Road
Street
Somerset
BA16 0PP
England

www.greenmagicpublishing.com

ISBN 978 1 8384185 6 4

GREEN MAGIC

CONTENTS

Paganism 7

Prehistory 10

Ancient World 23

Babylon 24

Ancient Egypt 26

Classic World 35

Greco-Roman Magic 36

Christian Mysticism 44

European High Magic 55

Neopaganism 57

Voodoo Veves 64

Theosophy 70

Thelema 75

Heathenism 79

Norse/Germanic Heathenism (Asatru) 82

CONTENTS

Slavic Heathenism (Rodnov) 119

British Neopaganism 127

British Heathenism 132

Neo Druidism 133

British Witchcraft... 142

Wicca 148

Goddess Movement.. 152

Nature Religion.. 175

Luciferianism and Satanism............................. 176

Neoshamanism... 184

New Age Movement... 200

Further Reading 218

Paganism

Pagan is a word first employed by 4th century Christians living in the Middle East, to describe people in the Greek and Roman Empires who practised non-Christian beliefs. It comes from the Latin - paganus, meaning rural, rustic or country dweller (yokel).

Early Christians originally used the term 'Hellene' to describe non-Christians. Hellene is the Greek name for Greeks, and as Christianity emerged in the Near East, the western, polytheistic Hellenes were used to differentiate between Christians and non-Christians.

During pagan times, all the cultures of the ancient and classic worlds only had customs, there was no such all encompassing word as religion to describe their beliefs. In medieval times, pagan was mistakenly believed to reference a religious sect. Paganism as a title was intended only to reference non-Christian and non-Jewish beliefs, isolating them into one solitary category that could easily be destroyed and replaced.

The term was revived during the Renaissance to differentiate the old traditions from the contemporary Christian faith, referring to various pre-Christian religions belonging to a number of ancient cultures such as the Greeks, Romans, Celts, Norse and Slavs. It was never used to differentiate between polytheism and monotheism.

In modern times, paganism is used to define a religion that worships many gods, especially those that existed before the world's main religions, specifically a non-Christian or pre-Christian religion - Hinduism, Buddhism, Daoism and Shamanism.

Many modern occultists categorise paganism into three distinct categories. Paleo-paganism is the standard of paganism, a pagan culture which has not yet been disrupted by civilization by another culture. Meso-paganism includes the native religions of America, Australia, Africa, Asia and pre-patriarchial Old Europe.

Neopaganism is considered an attempt by modern people to reconnect with nature, using rituals, imagery and forms adapted from classical paganism, adjusting them to meet the spiritual needs of people living in the modern world.

PAGAN SIGILS

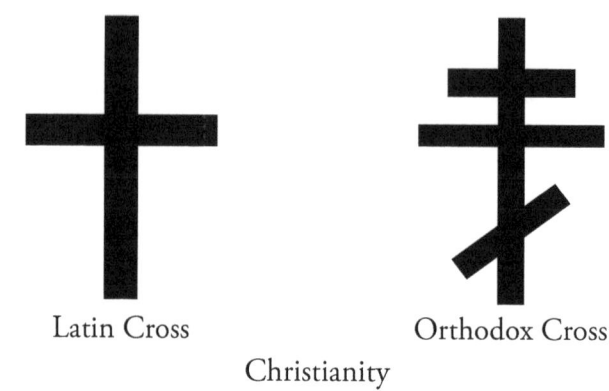

Latin Cross   Orthodox Cross
Christianity

 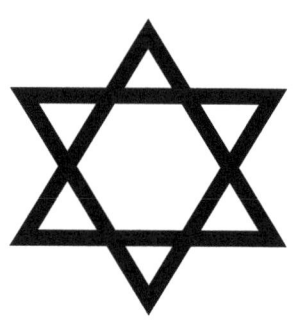

Menorah   Star of David
Judaism

Crescent Moon and five pointed Star
Islam

Abrahamic World Religions - Non-Pagan

Pratik - Hinduism

Khanda - Sikhism

Dharma Wheel - Buddhism

Enso - Zen Buddhism

Pa Kua - Daoism

Tome - Shinto

Non-Abrahamic World Religions - Pagan

Prehistory

Symbols are the way our ancestors took all information as energy and put it into symbols. The earliest date for the beginning of human mark making is around 70.000 BCE with tally marks used for counting the number of days travelled and for calender making, charting the periods of the sun for days, seasons and years and the moon for months. These marks were usually simple dot and line notches in bone and wood, called 'talking sticks' they are the first form of measuring devices, the origin of the ruler.

The oldest signs with meaning are the dot and the line, from these two signs all other signs are formed. A dot can be expanded to form a circle that can be bisected by a vertical or horizontal line to create two from one or represent the horizon. A dot sign can have lines drawn through its center to represent the four or eight compass points that forms a star pattern.

The most famous prehistoric art is from the caves of Spain and France, painted between 40.000 and 30,000 BCE. Most famous for their scenes of wild animals, they may also feature the first depictions of the shaman or even deity.

As opposed to the figurative art of prehistory, the concept of universal figures is even more apparent in geometric cave art. Such basic but meaningful abstract forms based on geometric shapes are the beginning of all written communication between gods and men, and men and men.

Following their discovery, it was theorized that they involved rituals of sympathetic magic designed to ensure a good hunt or they were produced under the influence of hallucinogenic substances during Shamanic rituals.

Another recent theory suggests the caves are filled with light during the Summer solstice and the paintings represent the zodiac created during the age of Taurus. An even more recent theory suggests that 32 of the many geometric signs accompanying such painting are repeated and combined in such a way that they could be understood as messages or even spells.

PAGAN SIGILS

Talking Stick 70,00 BCE

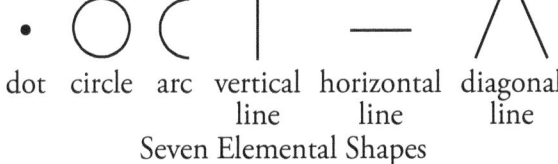

dot circle arc vertical horizontal diagonal
              line   line   line

Seven Elemental Shapes

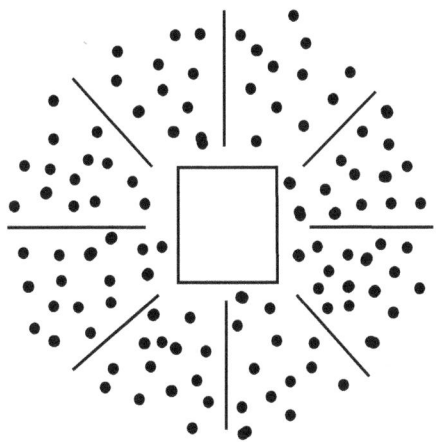

Creation symbol circa 30,000 BCE

Hunting Magic 25.000 BCE
Archaic Symbolism

Human Figurative Art

The human figure is represented in the earliest forms of prehistoric art from the sculptured Venus figurines and enigmatic cave painting of the shaman/deity of the Paleolithic to the Neolithic symbolism of Indalo.

Found throughout Eurasia, Venus figurines are tiny sculptures of the human form. Carved from rock, bone and antler or sculptured in clay, they are infamous for their exaggerated, sexual form as symbols of fertility and sex. They were produced over a period of 20,000 years during the Upper Paleolithic era, circa 35,000 years ago.

The figurines Their purpose is debated with opinion ranging from pornography to socially functional depictions of women.

Others suggest they imply the existence of a peaceful, matriarchal, goddess worshipping civilization in the Old Stone Age. Another suggestion is that the Venus figurine are not fetish objects but actually self portraits created by pregnant women as they see themselves. Although this theory does not hold for all the figurines from that period.

The Sorcerer is one of the names given to a enigmatic cave painting found in France dating from around 13,000 BCE. A copy of this cave art was drawn by Henri Breuil, who asserted that the cave painting depicted a shaman or magician performing a hunting magic ritual. Some scholars dispute this, claiming the cave painting lacks the antlers shown in the drawing, discounting the theory that the sorcerer was evidence of horned god that dated back to Paleolithic times. It is also cited as the first depiction of a deity.

Indalo is a Neolithic symbol found in the caves of Almeira, Spain, it is thought to have been created about 5000 years ago. The image shows a stick man holding an arch above his head, representing either a rainbow or the vault of heaven. Indalo was perceived to be a go-between between man and God, the rainbow providing a bridge between Heaven and Earth.

PAGAN SIGILS

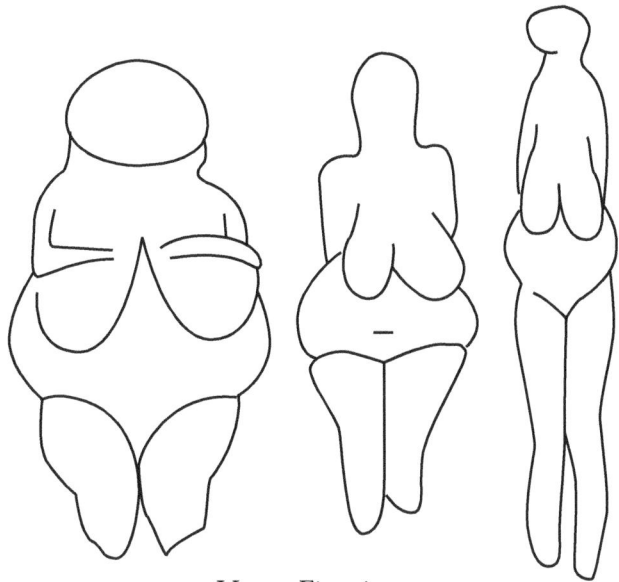

Venus Figurines

The Sorcerer　　　　　　　　Indalo

PAGAN SIGILS

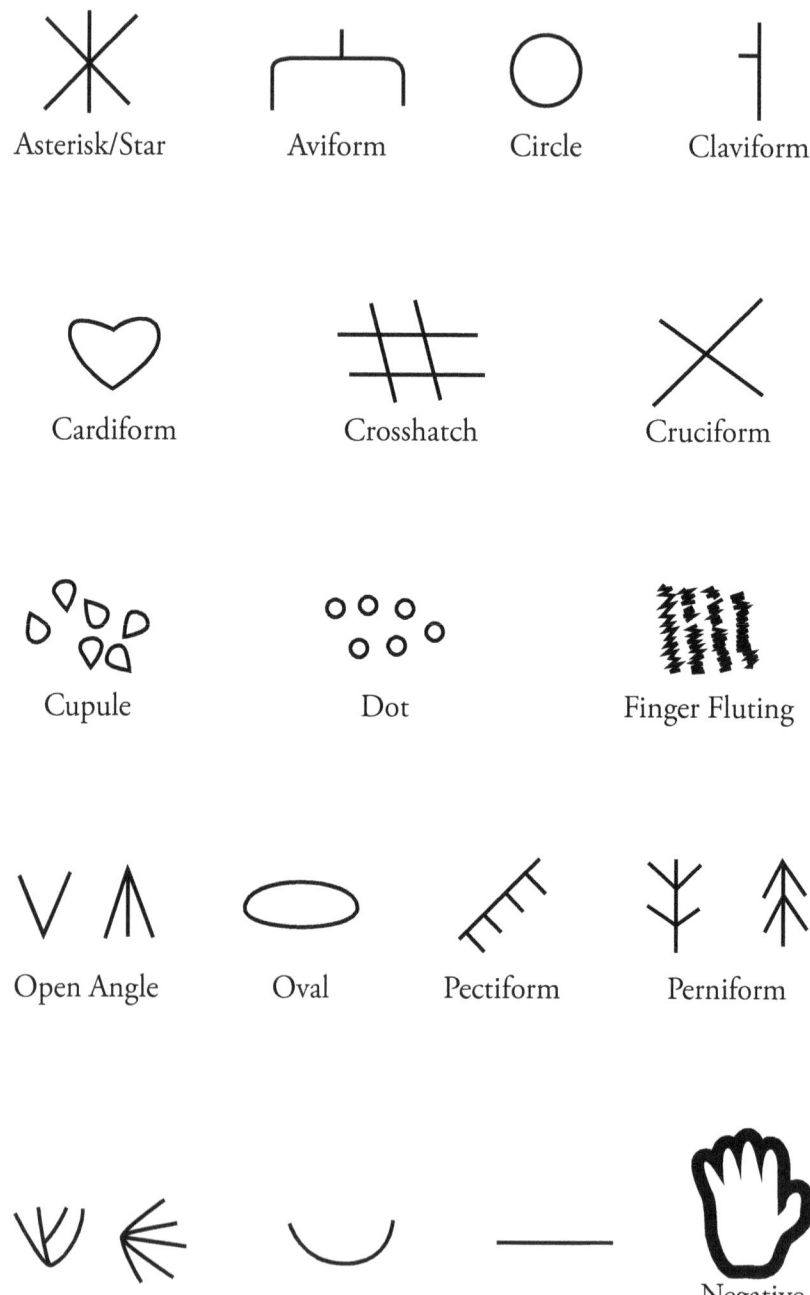

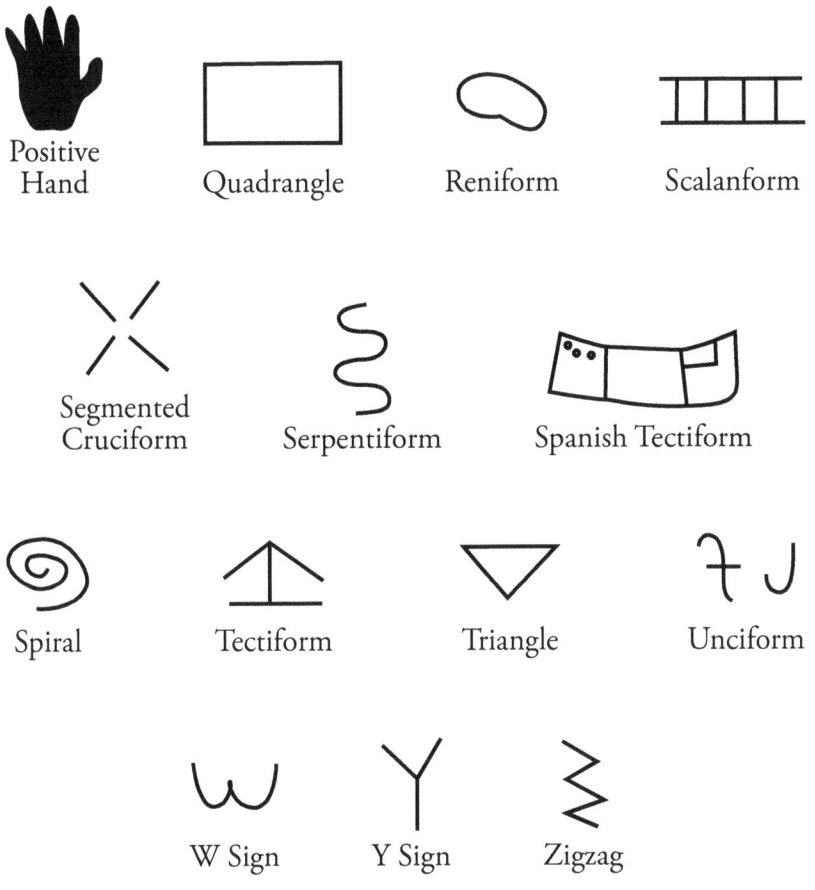

32 Meaningful Signs from Ice Age Europe

After examining hundreds of Ice Age cave sites across Europe, paleo-archeologist Genevieve von Petzinger discovered that our ancestors used 32 signs repeatedly. The oldest of which, a red disc the size of a saucer, is estimated to be at least 41,000 years old.

She compiled a data base of geometric signs found at the 370 rock sites situated across the European continent. The use of these signs spanned 30,000 years of human habitation and sign making.

A negative hand is one of the oldest types of imagery in the world. They are made placing a hand on a wall and spitting paint over it to leave an outline.

Symbolism

The mystery language of magic is symbolism. It is a language we all recognise but few of us are fluent in it. The majority of symbols that exist today were created long ago. They represent the movements of earth and heaven, the four seasons and representations of cosmic and earthly deities. Over time they have acquired layers of increasingly complex meaning.

All symbols are formed from seven basic shapes, variations of the dot and line or egg and sperm. The dot, line and circle are the most elementary of these. They are the parents from which all others have evolved.

The dot or point signifies unity, the origin, source or beginning. The circle is the dot expanded to infinity, symbolizing the universe, eternity, unity, eternal motion, the abyss and nothing. An arc is a bisected circle. The upper section is symbolic of the rising sun and the rainbow. The lower section forms the basis of all lunar symbols, it represents the feminine, passive, receptive principle, symbolic of the womb and the cup or chalice.

The line, drawn with a single stroke can be straight, wavy or zigzag. The vertical line is the active, dynamic principle, the body erect. The horizontal line represents the passive, static principle, the body supine. The oblique line is halfway between the vertical and the horizontal. A wavy line and a zigzag are not the same. A wavy line is fluid and passive, the zigzag is sharp, jagged and abrupt.

Universal magic symbols

Solar Cross

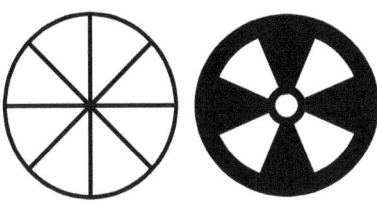

Sun Wheel

 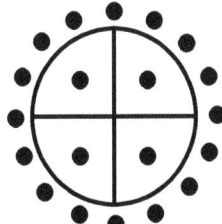 

Neolithic Sun Cross Bronze Age Norse Iron Age Celtic
Earth / Kingship   Thunder / Energy Christianity

Sun Cross

A cross within a circle, this prehistoric symbol first appeared between the Neolithic and Bronze age periods of European history, used to represent thunder, power and energy. In astrology it is the symbol representing the planet and element of Earth.

Because it was the symbol of the sun, kingship and the highest spiritual power, it was easy for early Christians to adopt this pagan symbol and incorporate it into the Latin Cross, as in the later versions of the Celtic Cross found in Ireland, with its arms protruding beyond the circle.

Spiral Petrography

Biform   Triform   Quadraform

Spirals

One of the most common geometric motifs found throughout the world is the spiral. It dates from the painted and engraved walls of the Upper Paleolithic to the decorated megalithic standing stones of the Neolithic era.

The spiral represents many ideas like the sun, life, path of life, eternity, creation, reproduction cycle or even a portal to the spirit world. It featured heavily in the religious art of the Picts and Celts, expressed in many forms.

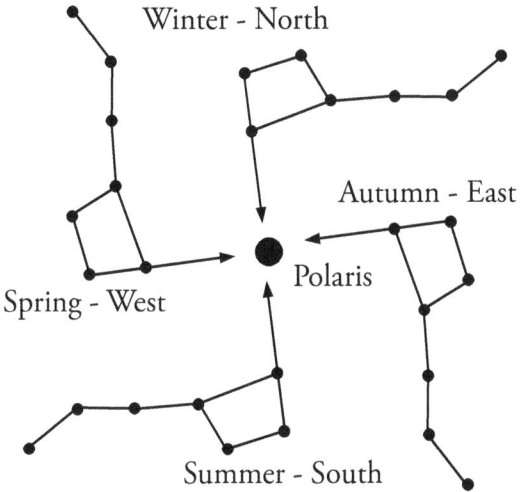

Celestial North Pole and the Little Dipper

Swastika variants

Swastika

The oldest example of this prehistoric symbol dates from around 15,000 BCE, employed as a symbol of fertility and regeneration carved into a mammoth tusk.

In Neolithic times it was common to all mankind as the Wheel of Life, representing the rotation of the heavens through the solar year, divided by the four cardinal directions and the four seasons.

Our modern notion of the sign begins with its Indo-European roots as the swasti, "sw - good, and asti - to exist" symbolizing the Wheel of Life, fertility, regeneration and good fortune.

After millennia of unchanged archaic tradition, the Nazi party adopted it as their logo, since when it has been culturally cast as a symbol representing an ultimate of evil.

Vinca Pictograms

A pictogram is a sign that represents a particular object such as the sun, water, trees, animals, buildings, tools and weapons, or actions like run, carry, wave, welcome, halt, give, receive, think, etc.

The oldest existing pictograms date to around 5500 BC, when they began to replace picture writing as the dominant form of visual communication. Called Vinca writing or Old European script, they were created by Neolithic people living around Vinca in Romania. The signs are found on a number of artefacts called the Tartaria tablets, found in Tartaria in Transylvania. These European pictograms are similar in character to the earliest Middle Eastern pictographic script, but predate such writing systems by 2000 years.

The Vinca culture disappeared around 4000 BCE and it is possible that their pictograms were transported to the first civilizations of Sumer and Egypt in the form of Astrolabes, star charts and zodiacs incised into clay and stone.

Around 3000 BCE, the first examples of pictographic script began to appear in the first civilizations, thanks to the invention of the Rebus writing system. Rebus writing employed picture signs and abstract symbols to represent words and syllables to enable the writing of names, specifically those of kings and short messages in dedications to the Gods and incantations.

These early pictographic scripts evolved into to the cumbersome hieroglyphic systems of the ancient world. Around 1050 BCE, the Phoenicians took elements from these ancient writing systems and the lunar calender to create the first alphabet, from which all modern alphabets, including magic ones are descended.

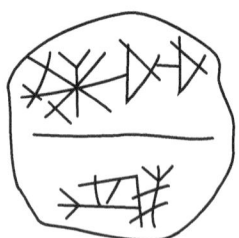  

Tartaria Tablets - Vinca astrolabes

PAGAN SIGILS

'Runic' pictograms of the Old European Vinca culture 5500 BCE

Common elemental letter symbols

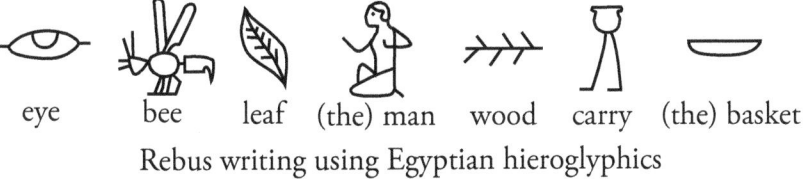
Rebus writing using Egyptian hieroglyphics

Ancient World

Without science the world was full of mystery, people asked questions like "who are we?, where do we come from?, why are we here?", which led to the creation of organized religion.

This time was the beginning of civilization and culture and it is likely that all magic symbolism existed before civilization and that technological innovations such as pottery and architecture were canvasses for the reproduction of magic symbols from prehistory to the ancient world.

The first great magicians of history were the priests of Babylon and Egypt, who were seen as the guardians of a secret knowledge given by the Gods to humanity to ward off the blows of fate.

The most respected magicians were those priests who could read the ancient books kept in temple and palace libraries. Only the ruling elite were fully literate, so written magic was the most prestigious of all. Private collections of spells were treasured possessions, handed down within the family.

Magic in the ancient world was predominantly aimed at maintenance and stability that involved a combination of ritual actions, symbolic imagery, performative recitation, written text, and appropriate material ingredients.

Many practises of the ancient world that we today label 'magic' had exact intention behind them for influencing the course of events to promote healing, offer protection, find love, and compel the gods and spirits.

Magic sigils were inscribed on amulets and talismans made of wood, clay and metal and worn round the neck or carried on the body. Commonly, they were depictions of gods, either illustrative or abstract in the form of their symbolism.

People wore pendants decorated with images and symbols to attract or dispel particular gods and goddesses. Just as a representation of an evil witch could be used to repel their magic.

Talismanic figures of another kind represented demons of such hideous form that it was believed the demon would flee when confronted with its own image.

Babylon

Babylon was just one of many empires in the Middle East that derived its culture from Sumer, the worlds first civilization. The Sumerians are considered to have been the first people to develop a writing system. It is thought that one of the major innovations in writing was the use of pictograms to write the names of Gods.

This culture was influenced by that of the Chaldeans or Star Gazers, thought to be very ancient Semitic peoples who settled and interacted with the native Mesopotamians. Abraham was a Chaldean high priest from the Babylonian city of Ur, whose ruling deity was the Moon God called Nanna / Sin, the Bull of Heaven.

By using astrological pictograms they managed to identify the divine nature of the Gods. The most often reproduced of these personal pictograms appear on four seals whose star symbolism was used to signify various members of the family of Enlil - Commander in Chief of the Annunaki Sky Gods on Earth, who was identified by the pentagram.

Enlil's first born son Nanna / Sin was represented by the Crescent Moon. Nanna / Sin's first born son Utu / Shamash was the Sun God and his twin sister Inanna / Ishtar was Venus. The seals used to identify the gods appeared on cylinder seals, pottery, architecture and protective amulets

Chaldio-Babylonian magic was the first system to attach planetary, celestial and numerical correspondences to the gods, to divine fate and destiny using numerology and astrology. It was also the first system to develop true names.

In Babylonian mythology, chaos existed because nothing had a name. So they conceived the idea of ascribing a numerical value to each sign in their syllabary so that every name was capable of numerical expression, this is the beginning of cabala.

Amulets made from different materials were worn around the neck as safeguards against disease, demons and misfortune. They were often engraved with images of divinities and always had talismanic formulae and incantations written on them. Magic conjurations included disrespectful incantations against evil spirits and the effects of sorcery, disease and misfortune.

PAGAN SIGILS

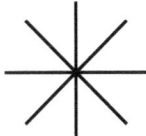 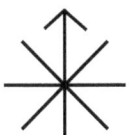

God / Heaven   Sky Father

Ancient Pictograms for God

Star - Moon   Sun - Moon   Venus - Moon

Planetary Characters

 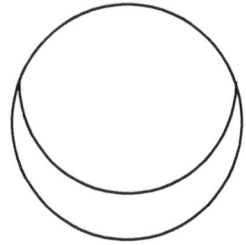

Enlil (Saturn)   Nannar / Sin (Moon)

Utu / Shamash (Sun)   Inanna / Ishtar (Venus)

Seals of the Sky Gods

Ancient Egypt

Religion in ancient Egypt was fully integrated into peoples lives. The gods were present at birth, throughout life and in the transition from earthly life to the eternal and continued to care for the soul in the afterlife.

The spiritual world was ever present in the physical world. This understanding was symbolized through images in art, architecture, amulets, statuary and the objects used by the nobility and clergy in the performance of their duties.

Symbols, in a largely illiterate society serve the vital purpose of relaying the most important values of the culture to the people, generation after generation, and so it was in ancient Egypt.

Peasant farmers would have been unable to read the literature, poetry and hymns which told the stories of their gods, kings and history but could look at an obelisk or a relief on a temple wall and read them through the symbols used.

Most Egyptians were illiterate and in daily life every class of Egyptian society wore amulets and talismans for protection. They also carried protective and healing spells that were written on papyrus, folded and worn against the body.

The three most important symbols, the Ankh, Djed and Was Scepter, often appeared in all manner of Egyptian artwork from amulets to architecture. They were frequently combined in inscriptions and often appeared on sarcophagi, together in a group or separately. In each case, the form represents the eternal value of the concept.

Heka was the Egyptian god of magic and medicine, and as in ancient China, the two were considered equally important. Using magic texts containing spells for treating diseases or injury, the ancient Egyptians used Heka or magic to empower hieroglyphs for amulets, talismans, magic figures and spells, created by priests, magicians, healers, scorpion charmers, midwives, nurses and protection makers. Among the magic doctors were Seers, people who could see the future. Seers could memorize spells for later use.

Was   Djed   Ankh

Strength, Success, Long Life

Was / Djed / Ankh

In ancient Egypt, the Wadjjet or Eye of Horus was the most popular symbol, followed by the Scarab, the Ankh, the Djed, the Was, the Shen, the Ajet and others. These other symbols were frequently paired or associated with the three most often used, the Ankh, the Djed and the Was. These symbols adorned the items Egyptians used in their daily lives.

The Was symbol represents a ceremonial staff held by various Gods, particularly Anubis and Set. It was a symbol of power and rulership, as is common with ceremonial scepters.

The Djet column represents stability. It was often displayed in combination with the Was scepter and the Ankh which created a combined meaning of strength, success and long life.

Ankh is Latin for 'cross with handle' and symbolizes the Key of Life. It is one of the most well known symbols of ancient Egypt, carried by the Gods in their right hand. The general meaning of the symbol is Eternal Life, corresponding to the soul instead of the body.

Wadjet - Eye of Ra

Wadjet - Eye of Horus

Wadjet - Neopagan

Wadjet / Eye of Ra / Eye of Horus

This Egyptian eye symbol first appeared in the pre dynastic period as the symbol of the protective Goddess Wadjet and remained so even though it was later more frequently associated with Ra, Horus and others. In Egyptian myth, the eye represented Wadjet as the Distant Goddess or was used as an aid by her and could take many forms. As the Eye of Ra, it symbolized her presence over creation and is said to gather information for Ra.

The Wadjet as the Eye of Horus is one of the most well known Egyptian symbols. Constructed of a stylized eye and eyebrow, the two lines that extend from the bottom of the eye are possibly to mimic the facial markings of a falcon that was local to Egypt, as Horus was symbolized by the falcon. The difference between the Eye of Horus and the Eye of Ra is, the Eye of Horus looks to the left, the Eye of Ra looks to the right.

20th century occultism and later modern pagans beliefs adopted the Wadjet and placed it within an equilateral triangle or pyramid, which it wasn't in the past. Most famously used by Aliester Crowely who saw it as representing knowledge, enlightenment and insight, particularly in spiritual and esoteric matters.

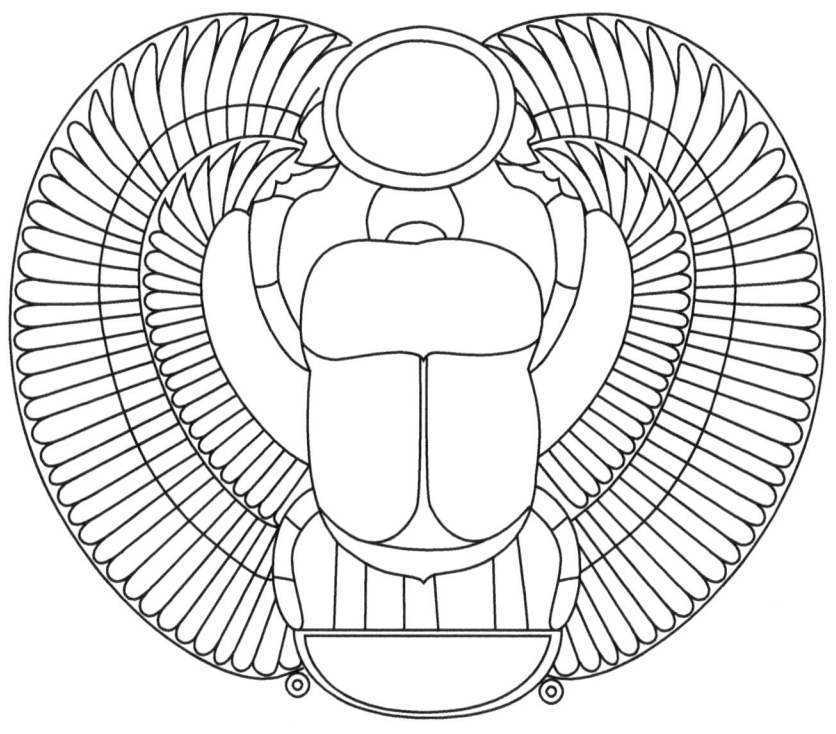

Scarab Beetle

The Scarab is one of the most frequently seen Egyptian symbols. The ancient Egyptians noticed that these 'dung beetles' had a practise of shaping balls of dung and rolling them to their nests to lay their eggs in them. They came to believe that the sun 'ball' was also rolled across the sky by the scarab headed God Khepri, who was tasked with the job of helping the sun to rise every morning and roll it across the sky through the day.

The Scarab wasn't used exclusively to represent Khepri. It was more of a universal symbol representing the renewal of the day, life after death, immortality, resurrection, transformation, creation and protection. Scarab amulets were very popular and came in a range of sizes and designs, some of which featured winged scarabs.

Shen

This sun symbol is formed by a simple circle with a horizontal line at the bottom. The circle represents a loop of rope with both ends visible yet tied together. The sun disc the rope encircles is a representation of the eternity of life, as the sun is central to life. Shen is derived from the word 'shenu' meaning 'encircle'. The Shen symbol is a representation of infinity and permanence and served as a protection device for rulers and deities.

Ajet

The Ajet represents the sunrise and the horizon. The Ajet is also depicted being guarded by two lions of Aker, the God of the Horizon. It was common to see amulets in the shape of this symbol to represent the sun rise and the rebirth of the sun every morning.

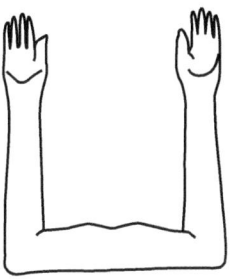

Ka

Ka is symbolic of soul, spirit, life, death, rebirth, afterlife, youth, vigour and eternity. Ka is the life force or soul given from the gods to mankind, but it still remains independent from the person, as the consciousness that could lead a person to the path of righteousness.

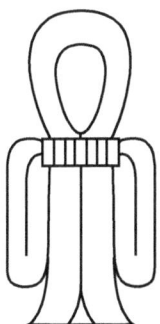

Tjet - Tiet - Tyet / Knot of Isis

Also known as the Buckle of Isis, Blood of Isis and Knot of Isis, the Tjet is a feminine symbol, thought to resemble a piece of cloth that has been looped then knotted. The symbol is found on funerary amulets, carved into the walls of temples and shrines and official palace seals and badges.

Some scholars speculate that it may be a drawing of the cloth used by menstruating women. Others say it is an interpretation intended to resemble the female reproductive organs. Others say it was intended to represent Isis's mystical powers of divinity. As Egyptian symbols had multiple meanings, it is possible that the Tjet symbolized all of these.

Winged Solar Disc

This symbol is one of the oldest in the world and variations of it are seen in many cultures. In Egypt is was called the Horus Behdety symbolizing kingship, power, the flight of the soul and divinity.

In Babylon its was the symbol of the Sun God Utu / Shamash. The ancient Persian religion of Zoroastrianism revered it as the Faravahara, symbol of Adru Madra, the Supreme Being.

Scholars think that Zoroastrianism helped to shape Abrahamic religion. Its concepts of a single god, heaven, hell and a day of judgement may have first been introduced to Jewish people during the Babylonian captivity.

Zoroastrianism is the Greek name for an ancient Persian (Iranian) religion that originated at least 4000 years ago. It was the worlds first monotheistic religion and is one of the oldest religions still in existence.

The Greeks had a fascination for Zoroaster who was perceived by them to be the 'Chaldean' founder of the Magi and inventor of both astrology and magic. During the Renaissance, scholars traced the origins of magic back to Zoroaster.

Egyptian

Assyrian

Farohar
Persian - Zoroastrian

Aten - Sun Disc

The Aten is a Sun Disc, originally an aspect of the god Ra in the traditional Egyptian pantheon. Pharaoh Ankhenaten made this monotheistic god the sole focus of official worship from his capital city and cult center of Amarna.

The redundant Egyptian priesthood despised Ankhenaten for replacing the traditional Gods with the monotheistic Aten and eventually brought his reign to and end.

His wife Nefertti and their son Tutankhaten ruled from Thebes for short periods after Ankhenaten's exile or exodus from Egypt, as Ankhenaten is though by some to be Moses.

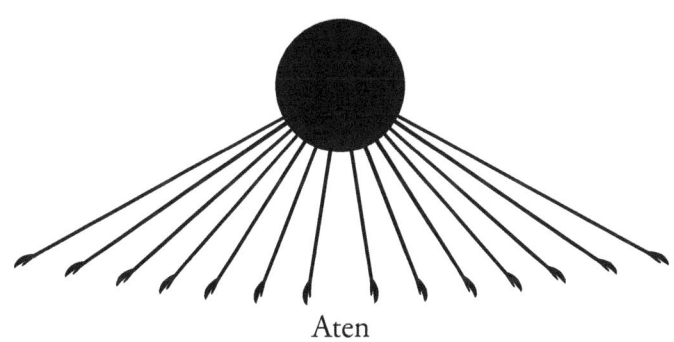

Aten

Classic World

The Classic World lasted from 1500 BCE to 500 CE and centered around the eastern Mediterranean area that included Egypt, Phoenicia, Greece, Palestine, Tunis and Rome.

Its early centuries saw the invention of the alphabet by the Phoenicians in 1050 BCE. Around 750 BCE, the Greeks adapted it to write Greek. Circa 550 BCE, Pythagoras used an archaic variant to develop his Cabalistic theory of Isosephy

The dominant culture was Greek with influences from the ancient Near East. It was the basis of European art, philosophy, society, education and magic. The term 'magic' came into use during the Hellenic era, from the Greek 'mageia' or 'magoi', derived from the Persian word 'Magi', the title given to Zoroastrian priests.

The Greeks and Romans believed magicians possessed arcane or secret knowledge and had the ability to channel power through any polytheistic deity, spirits or ancestors of the ancient pantheon.

Greco-Roman Egypt began in 325 BCE with Alexander the Great conquering and instituting the Ptolemaic dynasty on the throne of Egypt, which ended with the death of Cleopatra in 30 BCE. It was governed by Rome until 395 CE. After that, Egypt became a Coptic Christian country before the arrival of Islam.

In the Classic world, the centre of learning was in Greco-Roman Egypt, at the Library of Alexandria, instituted by Ptolemy Soter. The result was a mixing of ancient knowledge from India, Persia, Babylon and Egypt with existing Hebrew mysticism and Greek philosophy,, influencing the creation of new esoteric movements like Gnosticism, Neoplatonism, and Hermeticism, that contributed to the development of early Jewish and Christian mysticism.

Mostly written in ancient Greek but also Demotic and Old Coptic, Greek magical papyri is the name given to a large body of texts from Greco-Roman Egypt. Each contains a number of magic spells, formulae, hymns and rituals. They date from the 100s BCE to the 400s CE. The best known work is the Mithras Liturgy.

A common feature of these papyri was the synchronisation of Greek and Egyptian deities. Alexander the Great was seen as a liberator and pronounced as the Son of Ammon, or Zeus Ammon.

Greco-Roman Magic

Greek authorities and officialdom used and also feared magic but private individuals believed in magic. Farmers with their dependency on the weather, wore amulets around their wrist or neck to guarantee rain fall.

Greek amulets fall into two categories, talismans which brought good luck and phylacteries which protected. Amulets were made of wood, stone and more rarely, semi-precious stones.

They came in different shapes, miniature forms of the phallus, eye, vulva, knots, scarabs and obscene hand gestures, some of which are still widely used in Greece today, such as the Evil Eye.

Amulets were worn to cure physical ailments, attract a lover, fend off robbers, ward off the evil eye and protect the wearer. To make an amulet work, the gods had to be invoked, especially Hekate (Hecate), or make certain utterances that were believed to have magic power. Amulets were also made for walls, houses and entire towns and cities to protect them from any negative occurrences.

Curse tablets most often took the form of a thin sheet of metal, especially lead, inscribed with the curse and rolled or folded or even nailed shut and buried in the ground, tombs or wells. Spells were written on small pieces of papyrus or thin metal sheets and carried in a small pouch, or small container.

Rome worshipped many religions and people of all classes paid a small fee to magicians trading outside temples for love potions, charms, spells and amulets.

The Romans held a fear and ambivalence towards magic before they banned it. They introduced laws and practitioners and users of magic were persecuted and punished but they failed to prevent the populace from acquiring these objects.

Following the split in the Roman empire and the ascendency of the Orthodox Church, books of magic were burnt and the centre of sacred learning moved from Alexandria to Arabia and Persia, where the last remaining tenants of Chaldean magic became incorporated into Sufic mysticism.

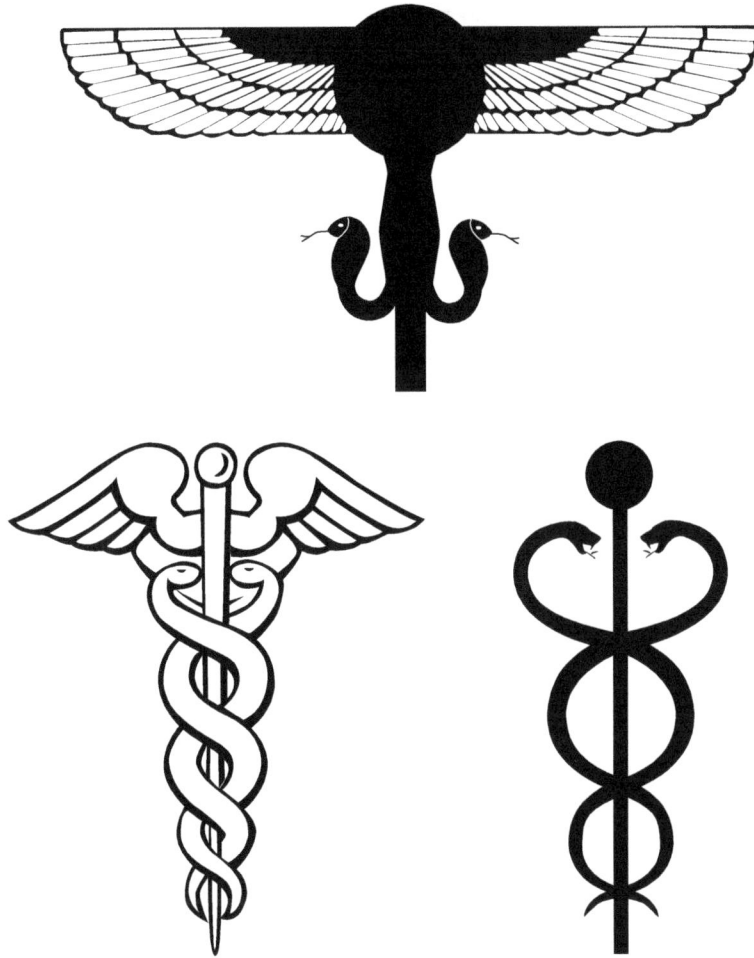

Caduceus

A very ancient symbol at least 4000 years old. As the emblem of the Greco-Roman God Hermes / Mercury, the rod or wand is the tool of all magicians, symbolic of the power and authority of magical and all supernatural forces. The serpents remind us of hidden knowledge forming an infinity symbol. The wings represent flight in physical and spiritual communication from heaven. The winged variant represents the Tree of Life. In the modern world, the wingless Caduceus is the emblem of the medical profession.

Ouroboros

An ancient symbol that first appeared in Egypt around 1600 BCE, although it is likely much older. Named by the Greeks it means 'Great Devourer' and speaks of motion, continuity and self-fertilization. Symbolizing not only the cyclical nature of time and the seasons but also the eternal circle of rebirth and eternity of Heaven and Earth working in harmony. In alchemy it speaks of wholeness and infinity.

Hekate's Wheel

This ancient Greek symbol represents rebirth and renewal. Hekate was a protective goddess who ruled over the earth, sea and sky and bestowed prosperity and daily blessings on families. The symbol is a circular labyrinth symbolizing rebirth, surrounding a center spiral symbolizing divine thought. Today, the symbol is used by Greek Reconstructionists and in Dianic traditions of Wicca.

Matisama / Evil Eye

Matisama is a Greek word meaning 'evil eye' often shortened to Mati or eye. The concept of the evil eye was widespread throughout the Mediterranean with its roots in Greece. Coloured blue, the eye itself is believed to be derived from the eye of a bull and can be placed within the palm of the hand to enhance its protective power. Its meaning hasn't changed throughout the millennia.

Saturnalia

The 13 pointed star is symbolic of Saturnalia. Saturn was the Roman god of agriculture and time. Saturnalia was his festival, the feast of the winter solstice. It began on December 25th with the feast of Sol Invicta (Mithras) and ended on January 1st with the Feast of Janus. To celebrate Saturnalia, people decorated their homes with greenery and gave gifts of wax taper candles called Cerei, signifying the light returning after the solstice.

Mithra / Mithras / Sol Invicta

Mithra was the Persian Sun God of Death and Resurrection, equivalent to the Egyptian Horus, the Greek Dionysus, the Syrian Adonis, Attis of Asia Minor and in Jesus in Judea.

His cult spread as far as Greece and Rome where he was worshipped as Mithras, a god of light, truth and honour with distinct differences between the Greek and Roman versions. His cult thrived in Rome, as the legionnaires God of choice.

Mithrasism was a potent religious force between the 1st and 4th centuries CE. His icons show him fighting a bull and wearing a halo, the circular sign for a supernatural force.

Chounubis / Ylaldabaoth

On many magic amulets in the Greco-Roman period used against stomach diseases, the multi-rayed crown or nimbus was found, usually in connection with the lion or leontocephaline figures like Mithras and Chounubis.

Chounubis is almost always depicted as being a man covered by a snake, serpent or dragon with a lions head. From ancient times, lions have been worshipped as animals of the sun. The Jewish god Yahweh is also often depicted as a lion faced anthropomorphic being, who was Lord of lightening, thunder and wind.

Abrasax

The God Abrasax comes from Greco-Egyptian mysticism, he is a 'word spirit', higher than God and the Devil, who combines all opposites into One Being. He is associated with influencing many of the first Gnostics who had gone on to form the various Abrahamic religions such as Judaism and Christianity.

The famous Abrasax talisman normally shows a mans body with the head of a cockerel, one arm with a shield and the other arm with a whip. He was engraved on gemstones used as amulets between the 2nd and 4th centuries. His magical name and its meaning are rooted in the secrecy of numerology, linked to the 7 days of the week and the 365 day solar year.

Hermetic Cross

Hermetica

Hermetica is a set of philosophical, religious and esoteric beliefs based primarily on the writings of Hermes Trismegistus or Thrice Great Hermes. The Thrice Great refers to Thoth, Hermes and Mercury, the composite Hermes, hence the term Hermetica.

The movement is generally traced back to the Greco-Egyptian city of Alexandria, capital of the Ptolemaic pharaoh's. Scientists of the time and their later counterparts considered Hermes Trismegistus as a wise pagan, a contemporary of Moses who foresaw the coming of Jesus Christ.

In Medieval Europe, Hermetica was seen as being opposed to the Church and became part of the occult underworld, intermingling with other occult movements and practises.

As a belief system, Hermetica unified elements of Egyptian occult beliefs (Osiris, Isis, Horus) and Greek Platonism with Jewish and Christian mysticism. The resulting composite proved compelling to Medieval Christian and Islamic scholars and to later Renaissance intellectuals. In particular, the notion that the universe operated on orderly principles which influenced the hermetical and alchemical treatise written by several people including John Dee, Francis Bacon and Isaac Newton.

Christian Mysticism

Christianity began in the Middle East during the 1st century CE, by the beginning of the Middle Ages circa 500 CE, it had become the dominant religion of the Romanised areas of Asia, North Africa and Europe. The availability of the Septugant or Bible written in Greek was a major factor in the influence of Christianity among the literate.

Although early Christianity is understood to be a Platonic philosophical prospect of patriarchal theology, there was a rich tradition of Christian mysticism that grew out of earlier Jewish mysticism which grew out of Hebrew mysticism which borrowed much from Babylonian mysticism, as Abraham was a Chaldean high priest. These beliefs influenced later Jewish teachings and Greek Neoplatonism which, in turn influenced early Christian mysticism.

The first Christians called their experiences of God 'apocalypses' or 'revelations'. The Book of Revelations mimics the form of other Jewish apocalypses's in which other worldly journeys of seers are described, focusing on the 'vision' or premonitionary journey and the 'revelation' of secret knowledge of world events and cosmic endings.

Much of the foundation of Christian mysticism can be found in the pagan mystery religions of the ancient world. From the Babylonian myth of the Sun God, Nimrod (Baal), who married his mother Semiramis who, after his death, conceived his son Tummuz by immaculate conception, is the belief in the Son of a Sun God conceived by a Holy Mother.

Its notion of a Supreme Being is Zoroastrian in origin and the idea of a God of death and resurrection was widespread throughout the Mediterranean, North Africa and the Near East. In Egypt he was Horus, in Greece Dionysus, in Syria Adonis, in Persia he was Mithras, in Asia Minor he was Attis and in Judea he was Jesus.

According to legend, many of the death and resurrection characters were born around the winter solstice to a virgin in humble surroundings with a star in the eastern sky. Some grew up to be spiritual masters with 12 disciples, performing miracles, giving baptisms and communion.

They all died but only three of them, Horus, Mithras and Jesus were crucified, before experiencing a miraculous resurrection. A similar story can be found in the Odinic mysteries of the Norse in the legends of Odin and his son Balder.

Christian bodies blocked the dangers of these parallels, perceived as threatening the 'Literalist' Church, by making absurd claims that the devil had engaged in 'diabolical mimicry', and plagiarization by adapting the story of Jesus before it had actually happened, accusing pagans and christians of diabolically counterfeiting the story.

Following the destruction of Jerusalem in 70 CE, Christian mysticism fractured into pieces. Variations included Orthodoxism, Arianism, Manichaeism and Nestorism. All of which spread as Christianity continued to grow in popularity across Eurasia.

To counteract this threat to Rome's power, Constantine made Christianity the state religion in 326 CE. He then oversaw the Council of Nicaea, where the Christian library was reduced to the books of the New Testament.

In 391 CE, Emperor Theodorus passed an edict to close all pagan temples and burn their books. Christian hordes set out on a murderous rampage across the empire smashing all traces of the mystery religions from which their traditions had blossomed, including the remains of the Library of Alexandria in Egypt.

By 400 CE, the Western Empire of the Romans had collapsed and fallen to the Vandals, Goths and Huns. Although the Dark Ages had begun only 88 years after the Council of Nicaea, the conversion of King Clovis of the Franks to Christianity in 496, marked the beginning end of European paganism.

Between 535 and 550, the Emperor of Byzantium, Justinian the Great of the Eastern Roman Empire, recaptured the Western Empire from the Goths. Within three years, due to the crippling cost of the Gothic War, Byzantium abandoned Italy to the Germanic Lombards. In 800, Charlemange of the Franks, a descendent of King Clovis was crowned Emperor of the Romans by Pope Leo the Third.

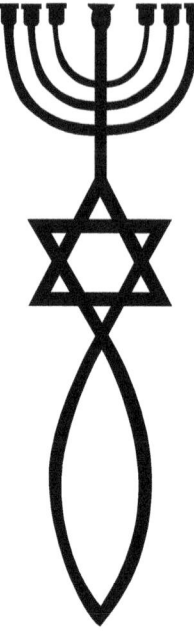

Messianic Seal

Judeo-Christianity / Messianic

The Seal of the Messianic movement dates from the 1st century CE, this symbol is comprised of three symbols, the Vesica Piscis, the Star of David and the Menorah.

The Jewish Messiah concept has its roots in the 'apocalyptic' literature of the 2nd century BCE. Centered around providing a future leader or king born of the line of David, who was to rule the Jewish people during the Messianic Age and the world to come.

After the death of Jesus, Christianity first emerged as a sect of Judaism practised in the Roman province of Judea. The first Christians were all Jews with apocalyptic beliefs, they regarded Jesus as the Son of God, considering him to be the Messiah of the Second Coming. They believed Yahweh, the God of Israel to be the only god. The Jewish-Christian community held faithfully to the Mosaic law of the Torah while accepting Jesus as the Messiah and mainly employed the Septuagint or Targum translations of the Hebrew scriptures.

Christian Sigils

The early Church Fathers established magic as an antithesis to Christianity by what is called the 'demonisation of magic' at the end of the Greco-Roman era. While Christianity drew on the beneficent divine power of God and his angels, all other rites drew on the necessary evil force of demons who were the Fallen Angels. Magicians by the very performance of their arts, entered into pacts with demons and so became agents of the devil.

From the end of the 2nd century CE, early Christians devised various symbols to represent the concept of Christ and their belief in him. These include the Icthius and a range of sigils called Christograms, that employed the letters of the Greek alphabet to create cryptic sigils for the recognition of their Christian faith, before using the more familiar cross, crucifix and halo.

The first important sigil of the early Christians was the sign of the Fish or Icthius, representing the Age of Pisces, the time of the Christian era according to astrology. The reason why Icthius is one of the most important early Christian sigils, is because it is an acrostic for the Greek phrase Iesous Christos Theou Hylos Soter - Jesus Christ Son of God, Saviour.

Christograms or Monograms of Christ are a combination of Greek letters bound together to form a meaningful symbol, a recognizable signature of the Son of God. Abbreviations of the name of Jesus Christ and, to a lesser extent, those of Mother Mary were used as form of shorthand and written in religious texts.

The first of these Christograms was the Tau Rho cross, also called the Shaurogram and Monogrammatic cross. It is a sigil that abbreviates the Greek word for Cross to, T - Tau and R - Rho, and is seen as a variation of the Chi Rho cross. The Tau symbolizes the cross on its own. Rho has the numerical value of 100, either a numerological reference to Abraham or the Greek word for Help.

Another term for Christogram is Chrismon which refers specifically to the Chi Rho (XP) cross. This sigil is a combination of the Greek letters X - Chi and R - Rho . They are the first two letters of the Greek word for Christ - Ch and R and together they represent Jesus.

The Chi Rho is often accompanied by the Alpha Omega symbols which are the first and last letters of the Greek alphabet. Together they represent the eternity of Christ as the Son of God. In the Book of Revelations Jesus says "I am the Alpha and Omega, the first and the last, the beginning and the end".

There were a considerable number of Christogram used by both the western and eastern Christian church during the early Medieval period. JHS was the most common Christogram in the West. Christians abbreviated the Greek spelling of Jesus, IHSOYS to IH, IHS, IHC and JHS. They denote the first three letters of the Greek name of Jesus, Iota, Eta, Sigma - JHS which is sometimes interpreted as Jesus Our Savior. The JHS surmounted by a cross above three nails is the emblem of the Jesuits.

In eastern Christianity, the most used Christogram is a four letter abbreviation, IC XC representing the name Jesus Christ. When added to a cross with the abbreviation NI KA it means Jesus Christ Conquers.

At the same time, the Greek for name Christ - XPISTOS - was abbreviated to X as in Xmas with the variants XP, XPC, XPS, XPI and XPM. The Greek letters IX, I - Iota and X - Chi represent the initials, JC for Jesus Christ.

Christograms for the Mother of Christ include AV for Ave Maria, MRThY for Mater Theou or Mother of God and IAMR Our Lady, Mother of God, Queen of Heaven.

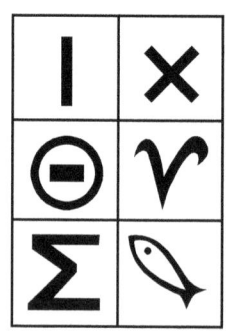

Vesica Piscis and Ichthys

PAGAN SIGILS

T - Tau   X - Chi   Alpha & Omega (First and Last)
P - Rho   P - Rho

Chi Rho, Alpha & Omega, Vesica Piscis

Jesus   Jesus Christ Conquers
(West)   (East)

X - Christ   I - Jesus. X - Christ

Ave Maria   Our Lady, Mother of God,   Mater Theou / Mother of God
               Queen of Heaven
Monograms of Jesus Christ and Mother Mary

Cross, Crucifix and Halo

Before the Middle Ages, the cross was common to all previous cultures. Since that time, its significance has been completely taken over and determined by Christianity.

In the Ancient World, the cross was a Babylonian symbol for the god Tammuz, an ancient sign of protection. The Ankh is the Tau cross of Egypt and this cross was revered among all ancient peoples of the world.

The pagan Sun Wheel symbol, as the sign of the highest temporal and spiritual powers, was adapted by Christians to incorporate the Latin Cross, whose ends protruded beyond the circle, to form the sign we know as the Celtic Cross. In the classic world, the Anchor symbolized 'safety'. The author of Hebrews adopted this symbol for the hope Christians have in Christ while they were still being persecuted.

Early Christians considered the cross as the 'accursed tree' a device of death and shame. It wasn't until Christianity was 'paganized', when the cross image became thought of as Christian. Crosses in churches did not appear until 431 and crosses on church steeples not until 586.

The quadratic cross is the archaic cross form and can be represented by the Greek letters T and X. The upright Christian cross is a T or Tau cross after the Greek letter. The diagonal Christian cross is a Chi cross after the Greek letter X - Chi, the initial letter of Christ.

When the quadratic and diagonal crosses are combined they form an eight pointed star, the oldest symbol for god, star and heaven. Various churches and cults used this cross to form their own unique cross form to represent them. The Fishtail Cross was adapted as the Cross of St. John, the Templar Cross and others.

The Latin Cross is a Roman adaptation of the Greek quadratic cross. It is the typical cross shape of the majority of Christians across the world. When the body of Christ appears on it, the cross then becomes a Crucifix, symbolizing life over death and the Roman Catholic church. The Orthodox Cross is a Latin Cross with two additional crossbars at the top and the bottom.

PAGAN SIGILS

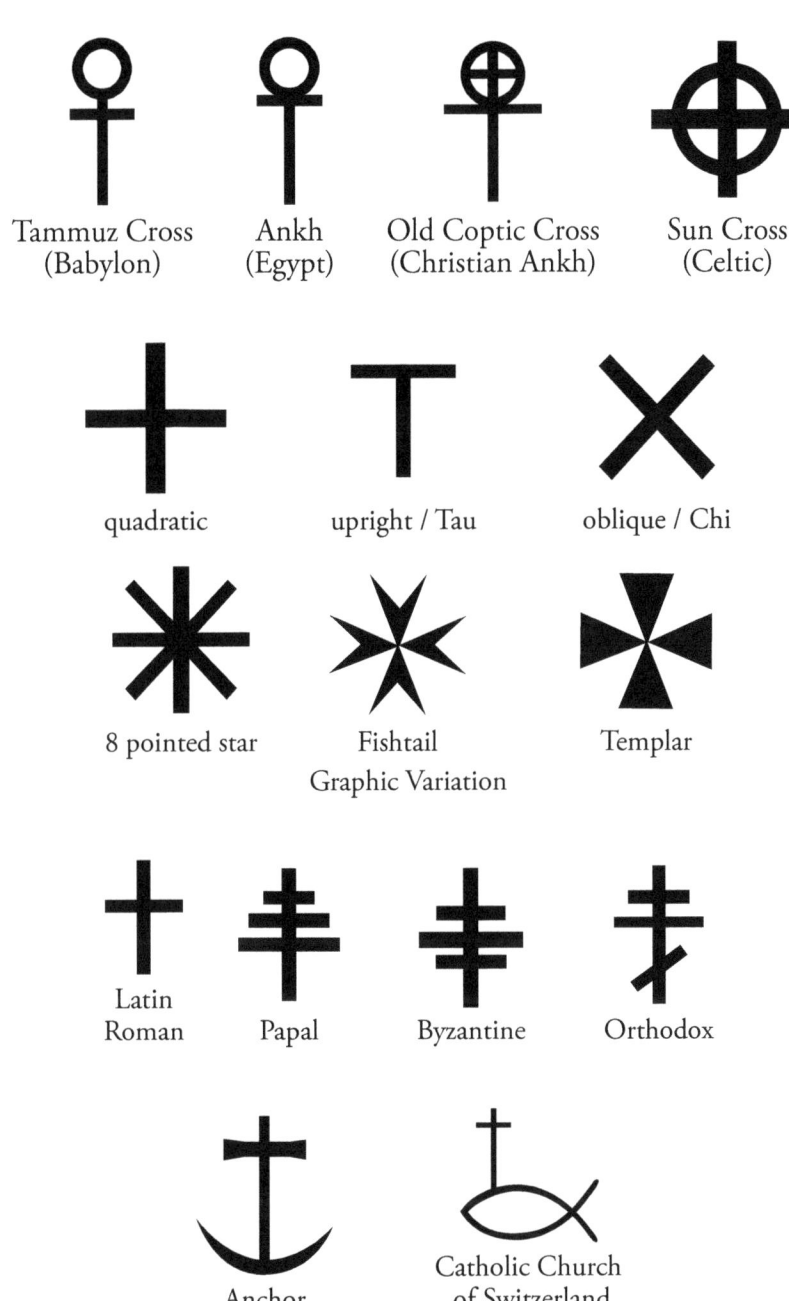

| Tammuz Cross (Babylon) | Ankh (Egypt) | Old Coptic Cross (Christian Ankh) | Sun Cross (Celtic) |

quadratic — upright / Tau — oblique / Chi

8 pointed star — Fishtail Graphic Variation — Templar

Latin Roman — Papal — Byzantine — Orthodox

Anchor — Catholic Church of Switzerland

Variants of the Cross

51

The top bar contains the initials I.N.R.I. and the lower, diagonal bar is the footrest, symbolizing Heaven and Hell. The 5 crosses of the Jerusalem Cross represent the five wounds of Christ. The Coptic Cross represents the 4 nails used.

Most Christians believe in a triune God of three individual and distinct persons, God the Father, the Son, and Holy Spirit represented by the Trefoils on the Eastern Crucifix.

Jerusalem / Crusaders (5 wounds)   Coptic (4 Nails)
Eastern Variations of the Cross

Roman Church   Assyrian Church

Oriental Church   Syrian Church

Crucifix - Western and Eastern variants

PAGAN SIGILS

The Halo or Nimbus is an ancient sign of a supernatural being or saint and associated with the Sun God Mithras as well as Jesus.

European High Magic

In the Middle Ages, pagan magic became synchronised with Christian dogma. During the European conversion to Christianity 300-1100 CE, magic was strictly identified with paganism. Christian missionaries used this to demonize the religious beliefs of the indigenous peoples of northern Europe, the Celts, Norse, Germans and Slavs. This demonization of non Christian beliefs and practises continued until the 20th century, ending with the repeal of the witchcraft laws in the 1950s.

From the Late Medieval era, beginning around 1250 to the end of the Renaissance circa 1700, Judeo-Christian mysticism mixed with Hermeticism, Jewish Cabala, Enochian and Solomonic magic, giving rise to the first grimoires and the scholarly occultism that would evolve into the High Magic of European occultism. Its primary concern was the ritual and ceremonies used in the conjuration of spirits by the magician. This is the form of magic that the modern mind associates with Black Magic and old occult practises.

In the Renaissance, the invocation of spirits using ritual magic was the focus of much occult practise, resulting in the publication of magical training books called grimoires. The most famous of these magical grimoire's, The Lesser Keys of Solomon contains lists of magic keys, sigils, seals and pentacles thought useful when invoking spirits. All such symbols were used in the construction of amulets and talismans which influenced the design of the Voodoo Veves of Haiti and the Icelandic rune staves called Galdrastafir.

During this time, it became fashionable to write anything connected with magic in one or more of the dead scripts from the ancient and classic worlds, particularly Egyptian hieroglyphs and Hebrew and Greek characters which, because of their antiquity, were considered to be holders of great magical power and resonance. Because more people were becoming literate in Latin, they were used as ciphers, to hide the esoteric knowledge condemned by the Christian church, although the majority of magicians considered themselves essentially Christian.

PAGAN SIGILS

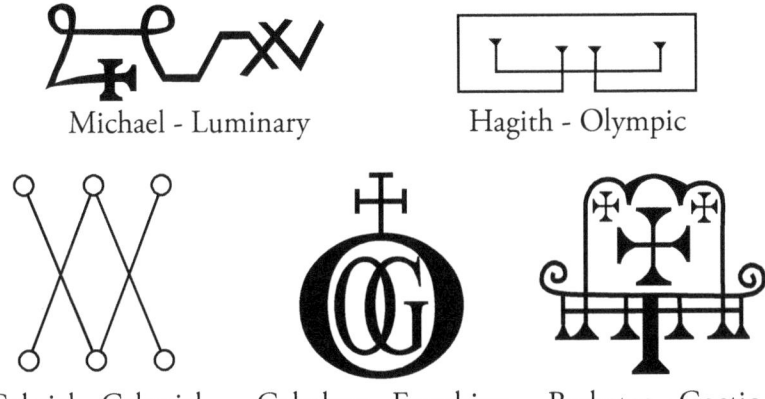

Michael - Luminary   Hagith - Olympic

Gabriel - Celestial   Galethog - Enochian   Barbatos - Goetic

Various styles of spirit sigil

Seals of the Sages of the Pyramid

Seal of Solomon   Secret Seal of Solomon   Mercury - pentacle

Solomonic seals and pentacles

Neopaganism

Neopaganism is a European, earth centered religious movement based around the revival of indigenous European religions that were replaced by Christianity, circa 1000 CE. Also called modern and contemporary paganism, Neopaganism can be viewed as a part of the much larger phenomenon of efforts to revive traditional, indigenous or native religions across the globe. This has led to religions such as Voodoo with its mixture of ancient African religion and Roman Catholicism to be classified as Neopagan.

Neopaganism is also associated with the New Age, the main difference between them being, the New Age focusses on an improved future, whereas the focus of Neopaganism is on the pre Christian past. What they have in common is the revolutionary concept of the 'Age of Aquarius' that provides both the New Age and Neopaganism with a millenniamistic metaphor which allows and encourages a framework for radical change in thought patterns and their means of implementation.

Before the 20th century, Christians regularly used the term pagan for everything outside of Judaism, Christianity, and from the 18th century onwards, Islam. Today, the term Neopagan covers a widely varied set of spiritual practises, adopted from pre Christian religions like Witchcraft, Druidry and Shamanism, and includes modern anti-Christian religions such as Satanism.

There are two main forms of Neopaganism, reconstructionist paganism that romanticize the past, and eclectic paganism that idealizes the future. Both aim to create a system in which humans can live in harmony with the Earth and its cycles.

Reconstructionist pagan groups are mainly found in Europe within Hellenism, Heathenry and Rodnovery, all of them prefer the term 'Native Faith'. They worship a pantheon of Gods, all of whom are considered to be of Indo-European origin. A minority have right wing views of race and ethnicity with some religions restricted to one ethnic group.

Reconstructionist religions are predominantly polytheistic and patriarchal, idealized revivals of Greek, Roman, Egyptian, Celtic, Norse, Germanic, Baltic and Slavic native beliefs.

Matriarchal Heathenism is the foundation of the native Cervanche people of the Canary Islands who are reconstructing the cult of the Goddess Tannit. In the 1990s, Middle Eastern reconstructionist pagans revived the worship of the related Semitic Goddess Asherah.

Eclectic paganism includes various forms of witchcraft, druidry and neoshamanism, some of whom hold New Age beliefs that embrace a universality and openness to towards humanity and the earth with religion, emphasizing a deep rooted sense of people and purpose. They worship the Earth Goddess and Horned God.

Originally, pagans looked to marry Christian theology with the old religion. Today, more modern Heathen extremists, in a time when political activists and New Age acolytes draw inspiration from these non Christian forms of religious expression, use paganism as a way of rejecting Judeo-Christianity which, as they see it, forcible outlawed their native traditions and culture.

The notion of paganism on the European mind became a inspiration in the 15th century with the availability of ancient texts such as those attributed to Hermes Trismegistus, that made paganism an intellectual position some Europeans began to identify with, beginning with those who wanted to form a new Greco-Roman pantheon.

The origins of neopaganism begin with the intellectual reaction to the 18th century scientific rational of the Age of Enlightenment, which led to the waning influence of magic on the European mind and the beginnings of the repeal of Witchcraft laws.

In tandem with this, the rejection of the Classicism of the Renaissance in favour of a glorified view of Medievalism, formed the Romantic movement of the 18th century, when peoples approach to paganism ranged from presenting the ancient Greek native faith of Hellenism as a powerful alternative to Christianity, to others who took an interest in paganism through the concept of the 'noble savage.'

The Neo Romantic movement of the 19th century saw a surge in of interest in Norse / German paganism with the Viking revival in

Britain and Scandinavia. The Viking movement began in 19th century Norway with the archeological discovery of the first buried Viking long boat, that produced new knowledge about the Vikings and their culture.

This coincided with a romanticized interest in European folklore which led to the birth of the Volkish movement in Germany. While Austria and Switzerland saw a rise in Druidism, being the heart of the pre Celtic Halstat culture.

Towards the end of the 19th century, paganism came to the fore through various international events and cultural developments including, new archeological discoveries in Egypt and a growing interest in Egyptian history, the rise of Spiritualism in the USA and the creation of New Age philosophies such as Theosophy and Thelema.

Combined with politics, these movements fostered an intellectual and spiritual rejection of the modern world, its industrial revolution, mechanization and consumerism. Eventually these aspirations cohered enough to become known as the Neopagan movement which lasted from 1870 to 1920 and was used to distinguish it from classical paganism.

The early 20th century saw the emergence of Neopagan movements in Britain and Europe influenced by the previous two decades. Some European groups preferred the term Heathen to Neopagan, as they consider themselves a reconstructionist religion, as close to the original as possible.

Inspired by the Victorian Celtic revival of the 19th century, English occultists returned to the ancient British traditions of Witchcraft and Druidism.

By 1933, German paganism had descended into the racial, ethnic and cultural exclusivity of the Aryan occultism that is associated with the ideology of the Nazi Party.

After the second world war, neopagans began to re-established heathenism in Europe and witchcraft and druidry in Britain. Partly due to the revival of pre war occult societies and partly by US influences, many of who distanced themselves from extremist organizations.

Post war paganism remained underground until the emergence of 1960s Counter Culture. During in this time, witchcraft was noticeably influenced by feminism leading to Earth and Goddess worship. This was parralled by the rise of Luciferianism, Satanism and the Neoshamanist movement in the 1970s.

Since the 1970s, Neopaganism has diversified into a wide variety of traditions. The 1980s were dominated by the boom in New Age movements when Wicca and Goddess cults influenced by feminism produced Dianic Wicca. The 1970s and 90s saw the revival of Volkish movement amongst extremist Heathen groups across Europe. After the collapse of the Soviet Union, East European pagans reconstucted the Slavic religion, Rodnov or Native Faith.

The establishment of the Internet in the early 1990s brought rapid growth to a lot of international pagan movements, including a rise in German Heathenism, followed by further interest in Asatru and Odinism in North America, Australia and New Zealand. This was mirrored by the rise of new Rodnov groups in the Balkans and Russo-Asia.

In the same decade, Faery Wicca and LGBT gender rights groups emerged from eclectic paganism. As does the Eco-Paganism of the early 21st century, which has its roots in Wicca, the largest of all the Neopagan religions with Druidry second.

Neopagans have no set texts or scripture and Neopagan symbology tends to be split into two groups, the revived symbols of reconstructionst paganism and the contemporary symbols of eclectic paganism. Some of which are inspired by the Chaos Magick sigilization technique developed by Austin Osman Spare in the early 20th century.

Among the most important of the revived and adopted images of early neopaganism are the Ennegram and the Yantra. The Ennegram is a nine pointed geometric figure with an open side, it is an ancient sign that cabalistic mysticism describes as 'the essence of being'. It was revived by the mystic teacher G. I. Gurdjieff whose teachings have had a far reaching effect on the last few generations of esoricists, using it to demonstrate his theories about certain cosmic laws.

Yantra is the Sanskrit word for ancient Hindu cosmograms and there are many such examples. This yantra is a temple symbol that has been adopted in Christian churches and Masonic Lodges. Formed of circles and triangles, the circle represents the world in which the living exist. The triangle pointing downwards shows the male Creator, the triangle pointing downwards shows the female Creator, distinct, yet united, they have a world within themselves in which the male is the uppermost. In the center circle, the image to be worshipped is to be placed.

When used, the figure is placed on the ground with North pointing East and South pointing West, then the relic of the Saint, the image of Buddha or a Christian crucifix is added to the center circle and the shrine for worship is complete.

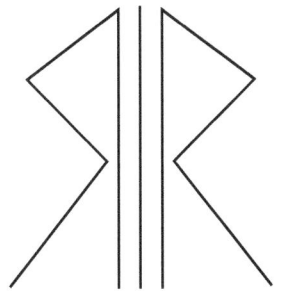

Roman - Reconstructed

LGBT - Eclectic

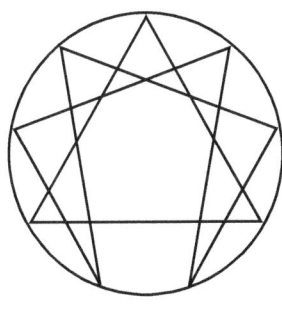

Ennegram

Yantra

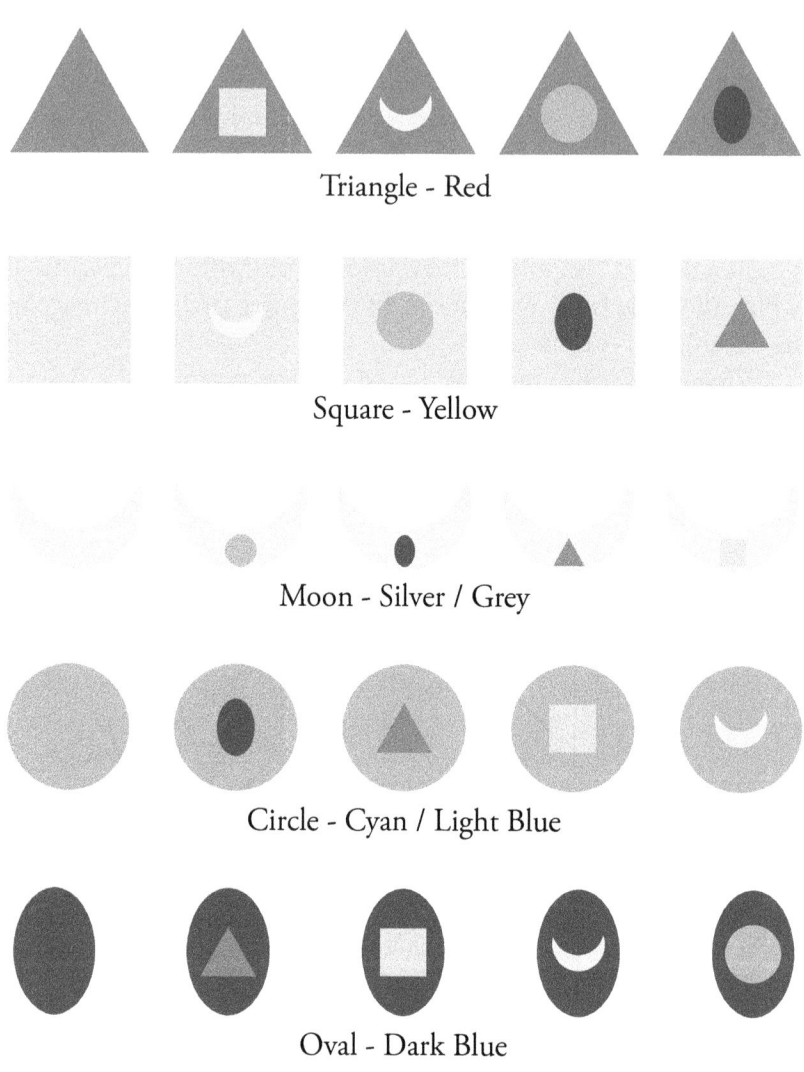

Triangle - Red

Square - Yellow

Moon - Silver / Grey

Circle - Cyan / Light Blue

Oval - Dark Blue

Astral Drawings

The fascination with mandalas and yantra's for European occultists was not the only example of the West adopting Eastern forms. Symbols derived from Tantric aids to meditation and altered states of consciousness were created by the Hermetic Order of the Golden Dawn. Using five elementary symbols they produced a set of 25 couloured symbols as an aid to visionary experiences.

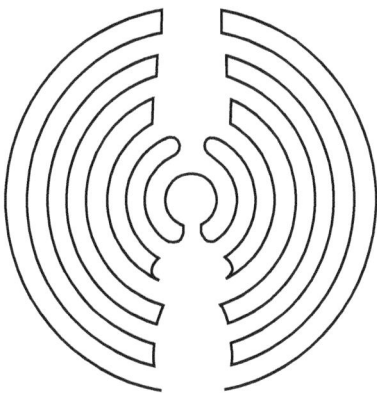

Dearinth

Invented by Oberon Zell as the symbol for his Church of All Worlds. Zell is credited with inventing the term Neopaganism. The symbol represents a labyrinth but also includes the figure of the God and Goddess. The nine concentric circles relate to the nine levels of initiation within the church.

Community Sigil

Sporane Pagan Village Community

Cross - positivity / Moons - finding your voice
Circle - community, sanctuary /
Star - tolerance / Pyramid - stability /
Pentagram - abundance.

Voodoo Veves

Voodoo or Voudou (spirit) is a New World religion classified as Neopagan. It is derived from the West African Voudoun religion of Benin, transported across the Atlantic ocean during the slave trade.

A monotheistic religion, Voodoo combines native African beliefs with those of European Roman Catholicism as African slaves were forbidden from practising their religion.

To get around this they began to equate their African gods with Catholic saints, performing their rituals using items and imagery of the Catholic Church. Some Voodoo priests confess to being Christian or Catholic Christian, others hold that the Catholic counterparts are primarily for appearance, not because the saints and spirits are one and the same.

It is primarily practised in the Caribbean, especially Haiti and New Orleans, where printed copies of the French, Grand Grimoire (Red Dragon) were taken and thought to have influenced the stylings of Voodoo Veves.

Voodooists believe in a single, supreme Godhead known as Bondye - the Great God. They also acknowledge the existence of lesser beings called Loa or Lwa. Believers provide food to the Loa in exchange for their assistance. Loa are divided into three family groups.

Rada are native African Loa who became major spirits in the new religion. They are generally benevolent and creative and associated with the colour white. Some Rada Loa also have Petro characteristics.

Petro are Loa that have originated in the New World, specifically in Haiti, they do not appear in African voudoun practises Symbolized by the colour red, they tend to be more aggressive, associated with darker practises. These Loa do not represent good and evil, as rituals dedicated toward assistance or harm of another can involve Loa's from either family.

Ghede Loa are associated with the dead, carnal practises and the colour black. They transport dead souls, behave irreverently, make obscene jokes and perform dances that mimic sexual intercourse. They celebrate Life amongst Death.

There is no standardised dogma within Voodoo temples, many teach different mythologies to appeal to the Loa, with some Loa associated with different families, Catholic saints or veves.

A voodoo veve is a religious symbol representing a voodoo Loa. They are drawn on the ground with cornmeal, wheat flour, wood ash, crushed bark, red brick dust, gunpowder or other powdery substances, and obliterated during the ritual.

Their origins are unknown, but thought to be derived from either the cosmograms of the Kongo people, or from the Nsibidi system of writing for the Igboid and Ekoid languages.

The Nsibidi system developed between 400 and 1400 CE, employing thousands of ideographic symbols, indigenous to southeastern Nigeria, used by Leopard secret societies called Ekper, also Ngbe and Egbo.

In voodoo rituals and formalities, veves represent the astral forces or Loa. Voodoo religious practices commonly include appealing to the Loa and inviting them to temporarily take possession of, or ride, a human body, so that they may communicate directly with believers. Sacrifices and offerings of food and drink are usually placed upon veves, to oblige the Loa to descend to earth.

Veves are considered to be the oracular alphabet of the Loa. Any other voodoo alphabet could only be an cipher for the Latin alphabet.

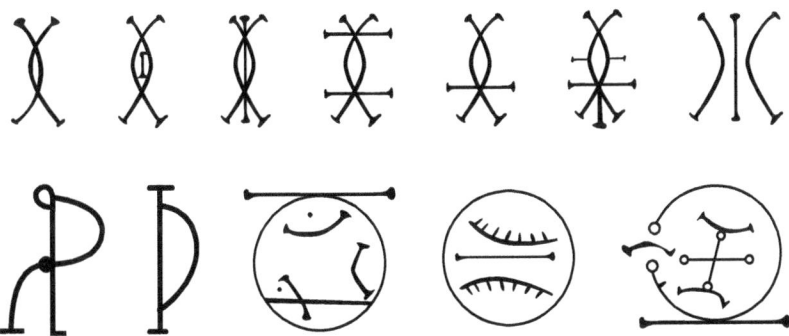

Nsibidi symbols

PAGAN SIGILS

Papa Legba

Kalfou

Ogoun

Freda / Erzulie

Ayizan

Maman Brigitte

PAGAN SIGILS

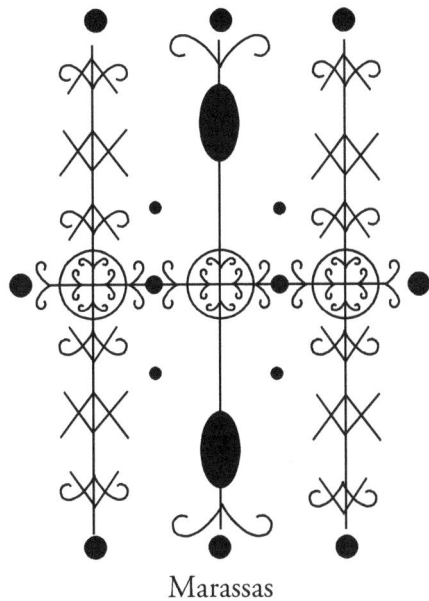

Marassas

Baron Samedi

PAGAN SIGILS

Damballah

Guede Nibo

Baron Cimetire

Voodoo Amulets and Talismans

Traditionally made from wood or clay, shaped into a medallion and worn around the neck, amulets and talismans have always been part of the African spiritual tradition. The most powerful of these amulets is the 'fetish' or Ju-Ju, popularly represented by the voodoo doll.

This tradition has not stopped and when Indian and Arabic immigrants arrived in Africa, they combined their own spiritual practises with African talismans.

And when Africans slaves were taken to the New World they brought their practises with them, secretly concealing it from their masters and Christian overseers, combing Voudoun and Goetic symbolism into their designs.

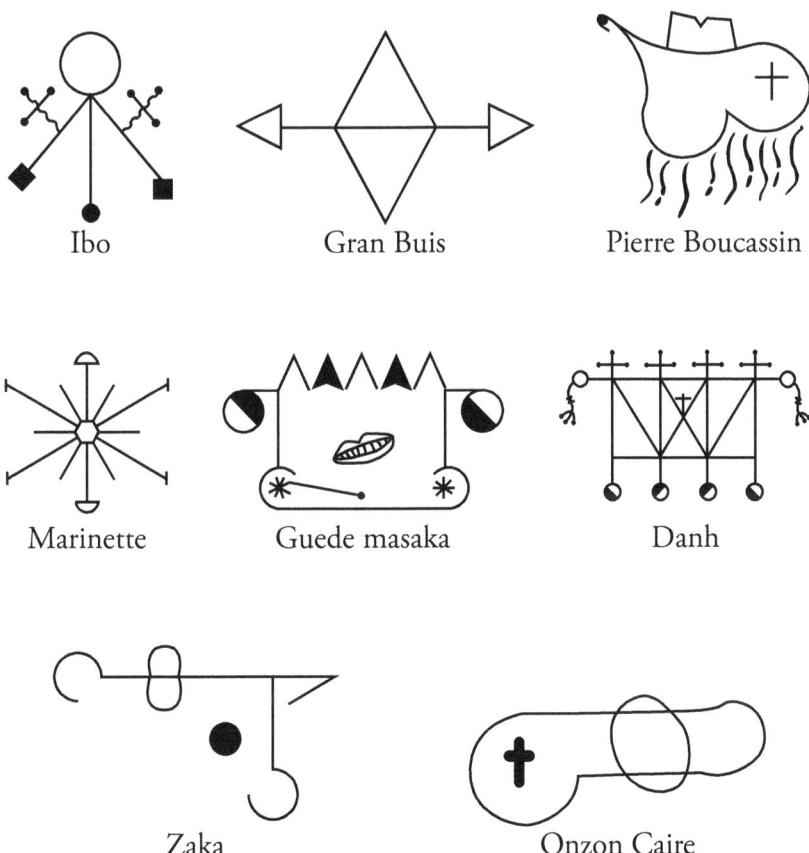

Theosophy

From 'Theos' meaning 'God' and 'Sophia' meaning 'Wisdom', Theosophy is a religious and metaphysical doctrine originating with the Russian born occultist Madame Helena Blavatsky and others who founded the Theosophical Society in 1875. Theosophy draws upon older European philosophies such as Neoplatonism and Asian religions such as Hinduism and Buddhism.

The fundamental teaching of Theosophy is the spiritual unity of all things. Rejecting the idea of God outside of nature, Theosophy speaks of an all pervading divine essence, an infinite ocean of consciousness, from which all things are born and to which they ultimately return.

According to the ageless wisdom, Theosophy teaches that the purpose of life is spiritual emancipation and claims that the human soul undergoes reincarnation upon bodily death according to a process of karma. The twin doctrines of reincarnation and karma make us responsible for our own destiny and prevents us from being the victims of change or fate at the hands of fickle deities and beliefs.

Blavatsky claims to unveil the ultimate synthesis of science, religion and philosophy based on ancient Hindu wisdom and occult Tibetan manuscripts.

She borrowed many of her ideas from Germanic mythology taken from the Eddas and saw Odin as an 'initiated master', one of the 35 Buddha's of Confession. She believed that the Ascended Masters are attempting to revive knowledge of an ancient tradition once found across the world and which will come again to eclipse the existing world religions.

The New Age movement has its roots in Theosophy, with its synthesis of the notion of evolutionary progress with chiefly Hindu-Buddhist religious concepts. Both the New Age and Neopaganism reject the notion of Maya or illusion, instead they fuse the notion of evolution with quasi-materialistic animism, perceived foremost in pre Christian European and pagan related religions.

Theosophical Seal

The emblem of the Theosophical Society is accompanied by the motto 'There is no religion higher than the truth' and is composed of a number of symbols, all of which have been use in ancient times to express profound spiritual and philosophical concepts about immortality and the Universe.

Serpent

The Serpent is the timeless symbol of the highest spiritual wisdom. Swallowing its tail, it is a symbol of regeneration. It is self-born, the circle of infinite wisdom. The circle itself is an ancient symbol of eternity and represents the absolute, the unmanifestated universe containing all the potentials of all form. As a representative of the Infinite Sphere, the 'World Egg' of archaic cosmology, the symbol is found in most world religions and philosophies.

Interlinked Triangles

The interlinked triangles, one light pointing upwards, one dark pointing downwards symbolize the descent of spirit into matter and its re-emergence from the confining limits form. They also suggest the constant conflict between light and dark forces in nature as well as the inseparable unity of spirit and matter. When depicted in the circle of the serpent, the figure represents the universe and the manifestation of Deity in time and space.

The three lines and three angles of each of the two triangles may remind us of the triple aspect of spirit: existence, consciousness and bliss, and the three aspects of matter: mobility, resistance and rhythm. The glyph is also the six-pointed star embracing spirit and physical consciousness, and viewed by the Pythagorean as the symbol for Creation.

Ankh

In the center of the emblem is the Ankh or Crux Ansata, ancient Egyptian symbol of resurrection. Depicted as being carried in the hand in Egyptian art, it is composed of the T or Tau cross symbolizing matter of the world of form, surmounted by a small circle representing spirit or life, with the circle marking the position of the head, it represents the mystic cube unfolded to form the Latin Cross.

Symbol of spiritual descended into matter and crucified thereon, but risen from death and resting triumphant on the arms of the conquered slayer, So that it may be said that the figure of the interlacing triangles enclosing the Ankh represents the human triumphant and the Divine triumphant in the human. As the Cross of Life, the Ankh then becomes a symbol of resurrection and immortality.

Swastika

The Swastika placed in the emblem at the head of the serpent, is one of the numerous forms in which the symbol of the cross is found. It is the fiery cross with arms of whirling flames revolving clockwise to represent the tremendous energies of nature incessantly creating and dissolving the forces through which the evolutionary process takes place.

In religions which recognise three aspects of Deity, the Swastika is associated with the third person of the Trinity, who is once creator and destroyer, Shiva in Hinduism, Holy Ghost in Christianity. Applied to humanity, it shows the humans as the link between heaven and earth, one hand pointing towards heaven or spirit, the other pointing to earth or matter.

Devanagari Sanskrit letters   Cursive Sacred symbol

Aum / Om

Above the emblem, in Sanskrit characters is the sacred word of Hinduism, Aum or Om. A word of profound significance said to stand for the Creative Word or Logos, the ineffable reality which is the source of all existence.

We are reminded of the statement, "In the beginning was the Word, and the Word was with God, and the Word was God", and that word was Aum according to the Vedas.

Thelema

As an esoteric and occult society of spiritual thought, Thelema meaning 'to will, wish, wait or purpose' is a religious philosophy based on the The Book of Law written by Aleister Crowley, that has parallels with Eastern religions, especially Buddhism.

Thelema was developed in the early 1900s by ceremonial magician and mystic Aleister Crowley. Born Edward Crowley, he changed his name to Aleister following a life changing vision that showed him the way to his spiritual vocation.

After becoming involved with esoteric groups like the Hermetic Order of the Golden Dawn, Aurum Solis, Ordo Templis Orientalis and Astrum Argentum, he gradually evolved a full set of beliefs which drew on Oriental, Egyptian and an assortment of occult practises such as astrology, divination, numerology, inner alchemy and necromancy or discourse with spirits.

In late 19th century Britain, there was a revival of interest in the Hermetic occultism that emerged in the Renaissance. Crowley was a product of this revival. Just like the Theosophists, Crowley was heavily influenced by Indian and Chinese philosophy and imagery but the magic practises of the Hermetic Order of the Golden Dawn included ancient Egyptian and Greek rites and imagery which was more appealing to Crowley. Crowley went on to be become the most influential figure that came to prominence in the early 20th century occult scene.

To a certain degree, Crowley's thought in general, inspired the rise of modern Neopaganism. He became a significant influence upon the founders of a variety of new religious movements and occultists including Gerald Gardner, the founder of Wicca and Austin Osman Spare, whose sigilization technique became the corner stone of Chaos Magick. Crowley's ideas also influenced the thoughts of certain Satanists including Anton Le Vey, founder of the Church of Satan.

Crowley's influence on Neopagan movements is derived from his Magnum Opus, Magic in Theory and Practise published in 1929. His definition of magic can be found in the modern witchcraft movement.

Crowley's interest in Egyptology stems from the belief in Hermeticism and Hermes Trismegistus being an ancient Egyptian. According to Crowley, the Law of Thelema or the Law of Will written in 1904 was dictated to him by an ancient Egyptian spirit called Aiwass, whilst he was in Egypt.

It laid out the key principle of life as Crowley saw it, the pursuit of each individual's will, unconstrained by popular opinion, law or conventional ethics. This concerned his major and much misinterpreted statement of "Do what thy will, shall be the whole of the Law'. He interpreted it as meaning "follow the true path to find one's free will.

Unicursal Hexagram

Any sign that can be drawn in one continuous line without the pen leaving the paper can be described as 'unicursal'. The five pointed star or pentagram being a good example. Generally, the six pointed star is drawn as a separate pair of interlinked, opposing triangles, but the unicursal variety was adopted by Crowley who perceived as an important personal symbol that has protective properties. It is also called the Magic Hexagram.

The points of a hexagram (male) and a pentagram (female) total eleven, the number of Divine Union. Crowley also added a five-petaled rose, symbolic of the hidden secret that conceals the pentagram within it. He used it as the emblem of Thelema.

Star of Babalon

Babalon, also called the Scarlet Woman, Great Mother and the Mother of Abominations is a goddess in Thelema, representing the basic female sexual impulse and the liberated woman, identified as Mother Earth in her most fertile sense. Crowley used it in his design for the seal of the Astrum Argentum or Silver Star order.

Cancellarius Seal

One of the symbolic seals created by Aleister Crowley's Astrum Argentum. As the name indicates, it indicates the position of Chancellor. The symbol shows an Eye of Horus at the center of rays that are set in 12 groups of 3.

Heathenism

Heathen is a Christian term used to describe the pre Christian, native religions of Europe. In the 19th century it was used only to refer to those who prayed to a Norse/Germanic pantheon of Gods. In more modern usage, it is a broad term referring to native religions of pre Christian Europe, predominately those of Greece, Italy, Scandinavia, Britain and Ireland, Germany, Eastern Europe, the Baltic States, Ukraine and Russia.

Prior to World War 2, German and Polish groups were referred to as Neopagan, today most of these groups prefer the term Heathen, as they consider themselves to be reconstructed religions, as close to the original as they can get, as a part of a tradition separate from Neopaganism, not a branch of it but a separate tree.

Modern Heathen groups are reviving and reconstructing such past beliefs, using surviving historical, archeological and folklore research from the Iron Age and early Middle Ages. Among the historical sources used are Old Norse texts called the Icelandic Eddas and Old English texts such as Beowulf.

Originally, Heathens looked to marry Christian theology with the old religion. Today, more modern Heathen extremists, in a time when political activists and new age acolytes draw inspiration from these non Christian forms of religious expression, use Heathenism as a way of rejecting Judeo-Christianity which, as they see it, forcible outlawed their native traditions and culture.

Heathens differ from Wiccans as magic is not essential or a central part of the religion. Heathens do not consider themselves witches, they have no degrees of initiation, no high priest or priestess and they reject the idea that all goddesses are aspects of the Goddess. Heathenism does not have a unified ideology and its pantheon centers on deities from pre Christian Germanic Europe such as Tyr, Odin, Thor, Frigg and Freya from Scandinavia, while Woden and Eostre are Anglo-Saxon.

Heathen groups share the same Indo-European mythology and symbology as other Neopagan groups, having their own ethnic or regional systems in which rune magic plays a central role.

To describe their faith, Heathens focusing on Scandinavian sources sometimes use the terms Asatru, Vanatru or Forn Sed. Practitioners focusing on Anglo-Saxon traditions use Fyrnsidu or Theodism. Those emphasizing German traditions include Armenism, the belief that the pagan past of the German people and their runic magic could point the way to a new religion of Sun worship and Irminism, the worship a pantheistic Teutonic God.

Those who espouse Volkish and far-right perspectives believe that the true Gods are those of the Germanic pantheon, and tend to favour Odinism, Wotanism, Wodanism or Odalism.

They believe that Heathenism is a religion only for those of white, northern Europeans descent. However, the majority of Heathens adopt the 'universalist' perspective, holding that the Heathen religion is open to all, irrespective of ethnic or racial heritage.

In the early 1970s, Heathen organizations emerged in Iceland, Britain, USA, Canada and Australia, largely independent of each other, due to a wider growth of paganism in the Counter Culture of the 1960s. Following the development of the New Age movement, further Heathen groups emerged in the 1980s and 90s, many of whom distanced themselves from the overly political agendas than their 60s and 70s forebears.

From the mid 1990s, the Internet greatly added to the propagation of Heathenry in various parts of the world. Many Heathen groups also began to interact with other ethnic-orientated pagan groups in Eastern Europe. The same decade saw the rise of racist Heathenry in US prisons.

Yggdrassil - Heathen Tree of life

PAGAN SIGILS

Thor's Hammer　　Fylfot Rune　　Gammadion　　Swastika

Broken Solar Cross　　Thule Society　　Nazism　　Neo-Nazi

Double Arm　　Greco-Roman

Fire Cross　　Thunder Cross

Spirit　　Soul
Heathen Swastika Variants

Norse/German Heathenism (Asatru)

Before 1800, German occultism was influenced by the Knight's Templar, Freemasonry and Rosicrucianism, all neo Gnostic sects. Inspired by the Romantic movements of the 18th and 19th centuries, German occultists increasingly focused on the religious belief systems of pre Christian, Germanic Europe.

The revived interest of the romanticization of a historical past with political implications, led several historical and occult societies to popularize this idea to a great extent.

The Viking revival movement was awakened in the 18th and 19th centuries. The word Viking was taken to refer to romanticized, heroic, idealized Norse seafarers and warriors.

The Geatish Society (Gothic Union, Gothic League) was created by a number of Swedish poets and writers in 1811. It published a magazine called Iduma which expanded its own views on Norse mythology as high art and revived the Viking spirit. The society was disbanded in 1844 after being defunct for 10 years.

Between 1880 and 1930, early German Heathens were strongly influenced by movements such as Odinism, Anthroprosophy, Volkism, Ariosophy, Armenism, Adonism and Irminism. A major influence on some of these movements was the Austrian occultist Guido Von List, noted for his interpretation of the runes. He used the terms German Faith, Teutonic Faith and the more archaic Folk Belief to describe a native German religion.

The term Odinism was first used in 1820 to describe the pre Christian religion of the European people of Germanic descent. It grew out of the 19th century neo Romantic movement through the work of individuals such as Austrian occultist Guido Von List.

In the early 20th century, Odinism inspired individuals like painter and writer Ludwig Fahrenkrog. He formed the Germanic Glaubens-Gemeinscaft (GGG), from out of which emerged the German Volkish movement.

Odinism had a second revival in the late 1960s and 70s, culminating in the establishment of the Odinic Rite organization in England, founded by John Yeowall in 1972 and expanded internationally during the 1990s and 2000s.

The Odinic Rites organization defines Odinism as the modern day expression of the ancient religion which grew and evolved with Indo-European peoples who settled in northern Europe and came to be known as Germans. The Odinic Rite shuns such descriptions as Viking religion or Asatru, insisting that the Viking era was just a very small period in the history and evolution of their faith.

The cult of German Heathenism began with the establishment of the first German Theosophical Society in 1884. In 1907, Rudolf Stiener split from the Society and along with other prominent Theosophists formed the Anthroprosophical Society in 1913.

Meaning 'human wisdom', Anthroprosophy aimed to make a scientific exploration of the spiritual world. It is notable for its deviations from modern science which includes racial evolution, clairvoyance and the myths of Atlantis.

Criticizing the Jewish roots of Christianity in 1900, Ernest Wachier published a pamphlet calling for the revival of a racialized, ancient German religion, leading to the formation of various German religious communities in 1911 and 1912. The racist elitist Pan German movement of ethnic German and Austrians was a reaction to the exclusion of Austria from Otto Von Bismark's German empire.

These developments ran in tandem with a growing notions of nationalism, socialism and the idea of 'folk', which combined to form the Volkish movement, established just after WW1. The Volkish movement was a sort of anti modern and anti liberal reaction to the many political, social and economic changes of life in 19th century Germany.

A development of the Volkish movement was Ariosophy, whose membership included Guido Von List. He established a religion called Wotanism with an inner core called Armenism that was heavily influenced by Theosophy.

Von List's work was transmitted in Germany by prominent right-wingers, and his adherents were founders of the Reichshammerbund in 1912. It included individuals who held key positions in the Germanemorden, a Volkish secret society whose aim was to monitor the Jews and spread anti-Semitism.

The Volkish movement also established itself in 1930s Norway with such groups as the Ragnarok Circle and others.

The Thule society developed from the Volkish Germanemorden, which sponsored and contained many members of the formative Nazi Party. The Thule society grew out of Von List's occultism and displayed a Theosophical influenced interpretation of Norse mythology and influenced the use of revived Indo-European symbols in the political and military insignia of the Nazi's.

The Thule society has become the center of many conspiracy theories concerning Nazi Germany including the creation of Vril-powered UFO's. After his rise to power, Hitler discouraged such occult pursuits. The Volkish and Thule Societies were dissolved and all occult organizations were oppressed by the Nazi regime through their anti freemasonry act of 1935.

Ariosophy and Armenanism were pioneered by Guido Von List and Jorg Franz Von Libenfries in Austria between 1890 to 1930. Ariosophy means wisdom of the Aryans and is a modern interpretation used to describe a subset of Aryan esoteric themes. The prevailing view of the time was called Armenanism created by Von List, while Libenfries used the term Theozoology and Ario-Chritianity before WW1.

Ariososphy is a racist occult movement that became a major strand of nationalist esotericism in Germany and Austria during the late 1800s and early 1900s and there were possible links between Arisosophy and Nazism. The Ariosophical movement took Volkish ideas and added occult forms like Freemasonry, Cabala and Rosicrucianism in order to prove the world is bad and based on fake and evil principles. Ariosophist ideas and symbols filtered through to several anti Semitic and nationalist groups from which the Nazi Party emerged.

The ideas of Von List and Libenfries were part of a general occult revival that occurred in Austria and Germany during the late 19th and early 20th century. A revival loosely inspired by historical German paganism and holistic philosophy, as well as esoteric concepts that were influenced by German Romanticism and Theosophy.

The connection between this form of German mysticism and historical German culture is evident in the mystical fascination with runes in the form of Von List's Armenan runes.

In 1925, Czech extremist Franz Sattier founded Adonism, devoted to the Greek God Adonis, who Sattier equated with the Christian Satan. Adonism died out during the 1930s but remained an influence on the German occult scene.

Irmininsm comes from the writings of Karl Maria Wiligut, an Austrian WW1 veteran and SS officer prior to WW2. As part of his position he was spiritual advisor to Hienrich Himmler, who incorporated Wiligut's teaching's into SS ritual's, preferring Irminism to Odinism or Volkish.

Reconstructed from various sources including linguistic and literary sources, Irminism began as a current of Ariosophy based on a Germanic deity called Irmin. In Old Saxon, the term is synonymous with the words 'great' and 'strong'. As such it was used as an epithet for the Gods such as Tyr and Odin. Irminism is a pantheistic concept meaning 'all within God', as opposed to Odinism which is polytheistic meaning 'many Gods'.

According to Wiligut, the German people are descended from Teut, progenitor of the Teutons. This tradition stretches back to the late Neolithic period when the Aryans first entered Europe. According to Wiligut, the ancient Tuetons prayed only to God or Got and to their ancestors. This gave Christians the false impression of Teutonic idolatry, as the Greeks and Romans had a tradition of hard polytheism and viewed their Gods as separate beings, not as individual aspects of the deity.

In 1933, the German Faith Movement was founded to unite these Heathen groups in the hope it would become the official faith of Nazi Germany but failed to do so.

The Volkish movement largely disappeared following Nazi Germany's defeat in WW2, only to reappear in the 1970s and 1990s with the rise of the Neo Nazi movement, while many of the Heathen groups who disbanded during the Nazi era reformed in the new West Germany.

Asatru is a Heathen religion translated as 'faith in the Gods' and its practitioners are called Asatruars. It is based on the Old Norse beliefs found in the Icelandic texts called the Eddas, involving the worship of the ancient Norse pantheon of gods and spirits, as opposed to the Germanic pantheon.

As a religion, Asatru has no fixed dogma or theology but the high priests have tended towards a polytheistic world view and distance themselves from the more politically extreme versions of Heathenism.

Since the 16th century, there had been an increasing interest in the revival of the pre Christian, native faith in Iceland. In the 1960s and 70s, native Icelanders began to re-institute Asatru, the Old Norse pagan religion of the islands original Viking settlers, abandoned in favour Christianity around 1000 CE.

It received special impetus, recognized by the Icelandic government in 1973, prompting several organizations to appear in Norway, Sweden, Denmark, Finland, North America and Australia.

This led to Astratu receiving a wide number of names with the same or similar meaning, Forn Sior - ancient religion or tradition, Forn Sed - old custom, Hedensk - pagan custom, Nordisk - Nordic custom. Others include The Elder Troth - The Old Way, Var Sior - Our Way, Norse Heathenism, Germanic Heathenism, and Folkish Asatru, the successor to the Viking Brotherhood, a US Heathen group founded by Steve McNahien in 1972.

During the 1970s and 80s, the term Asatru became a popular alternative to the term Heathenism, although this has diminished somewhat. The term Asatru is still in popular use among the descendents of Scandinavian immigrants living in North America and Australia.

Many racist orientated Heathen groups of the New World prefer the term Odinism, while Asatru is used by more moderate groups, who reject the corruptions that divides people into categories, but neither are distinguished from each other.

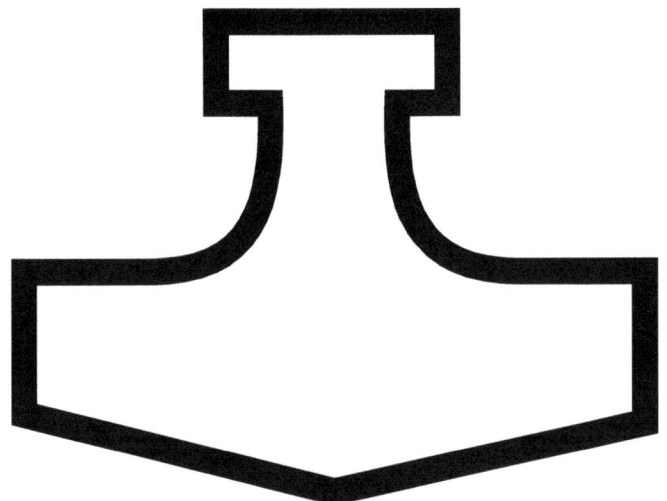

Mjolnir

Also known as Thor's Hammer and Hammer of the Gods, the Mjolnir symbol owes its significance to its long history as a supernaturally powerful object. The word carries with it connotations of crushing and grinding, both in an agricultural sense (it shares its roots with the word 'meal') and in the destructive sense. Both the hammer and the axe are associated with lightning because, like lightning they strike fast and hard. Thor as the God of Thunder found lightning to be a useful and appropriate weapon.

The origins of this particular hammer are steeped in myth. One legend describes it as having fallen to earth as a meteor, other sources state that the trickster god Loki manufactured it. Its power was legendary too, Mjolnir was able to destroy mountains or topple giants with a single strike. A particular feature of the hammer, which made it useful as a weapon of war, was its boomerang-like quality of returning to who ever threw it.

As an amulet, Mjolnir offers protection and despite its origins that are squarely placed within the pagan realms, it has managed to slip the net cast by Christianity. It continues to be popular today as a major symbol of the Asatru faith.

Horns of Odin (Triskele)

Norse legends tell of a magical mead brewed from the blood of Kvasir, a wise god. To drink this mead would be to benefit from the wisdom of the god. Odin managed to find this drink, and the triple horns represent the three draughts that he drank. Today the symbol is used as a sign of identity by followers of the Asatru faith.

Valknut / Odin's Knot

The Valknut consists of three interlocking triangles and has some similarity to the triquetra or the triskelle. The Valknut is of Viking origin and is seen on rune stones and in carvings and is connected with the God Odin. The name means roughly, Knot of Death or Knot of the Slain. The knot is believed to be a protective device, a quality shared by other knot symbols.

Gungir / Odin's Spear

Gungir is the name of the magical spear used in battle against the Vanir by the God Odin. It symbolizes power, protection, authority. Also called the Eternal Spear or the Declaration of Lord God, Gungir flew straight and never missed its target, penetrating and killing everything it was aimed at.

Black Sun

Also called the Sonnenrad or Sun Wheel, this archaic looking bind rune first appeared on the floor of the North Tower of Wewelsburg after Himmler ordered it to be remodelled. Based on a medieval design of dark green marble set in a cream coloured marble floor.

An invention of Nazi occultists, it is composed of 12 sig runes and was given the name "Black Sun" by Wilhelm Hanslig of the Landig Group. It is still used by Nazi occultists and has been adopted by Neo Nazi's and Satanists. It has negative associations with Night Sun and Dark Sun.

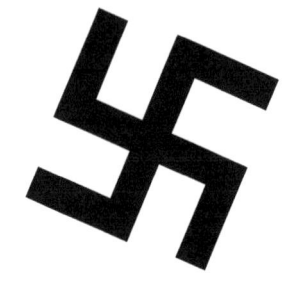 

Swastika - Hindu (Nazi Party)   Gamma Cross - Gk (Luftwaffe)

Nazi Aryan Symbols

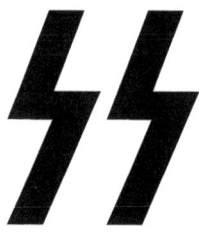  

Double Sig   Odal   Wolfsangel
victory   blood, unity   liberty, independence

Algiz   Eihwaz   Tyr   Hagel   Ger
Life   Death   Leadership   Nazi Faith   Community
                                              Spirit

SS Runes

The Runic insignia of the Shutzstaffell or SS runen were used from the 1920s to 1945. They appeared on SS flags, uniforms and other items as symbols of various aspects of Nazi ideology and German mysticism. They also represented virtues seen as desirable in SS members.

Rune Magic

Central to the mystical beliefs of Heathenism is the notion of Rune Magic. Germanic ancestral lore sings of an ancient tribe known as the Volsungr, who wandered out of the far north with the last great Ice Age. They were the guardians of the primordial forests and ancient track ways. It was also the task of the Volsungr to seed the knowledge of the runes among the newer tribes who would maintain their mysteries. Once this task was complete they withdrew into deepest, holiest Northern forests and passed beyond human knowledge.

In the European pagan mystical tradition, runes were employed as mystic symbol system before they were adapted into a writing system. Tacitus recorded in 98 AD that Drottirs or Germanic druids were taking auspices and casting lots using runes. He says that Druids cast lots using rune symbols incised on to discs of nut wood or pebbles and coloured red. These were thrown at random into a white cloth whilst the Gods were invoked. The priest took three sticks or stones, one at a time from the cloth, interpreting the sigils accordingly. Blotspann it the name given to the method of divination which involves casting three wooden chips inscribed with runes into a bowl containing the blood of sacrificed animals to obtain warnings and see into the future.

The runes were not invented, they were and are seen as pre-existing forces handed down from eternity. They are considered intrinsically magic by their very nature. They promoted communication, not only between men but between mankind and deities, allowing for a conversation with the hidden powers that animate the world. Each runic character has several attributes, an alphabetical value, a numerical value, a pictorial representation (Fehu is based on the depiction of a cattle skull), a divinatory one, an aural one (the chanting or singing of the runes name for meditation and prayer), and a definitive one.

In the Germanic Iron Age, magic runes such as Sig and Tyr are mentioned as being carved on swords in Medieval sources such as the Eddas. Rune magic was used as a form of protection, to cast spells, cure illness, attract love and fortune. Runes used to foretell the future are called prophetic runes.

Runes can be arranged together to form Bind Runes. Binding runes increases their power and creates magic formulas. The most complicated of bind runes are the 17th century Icelandic rune staves called Galdrastafir, a mixture of Viking and Christian magic.

In the early 20th century, German mystics coined the phrase 'rune magic' and developed new forms including the revived form of the Elder Futhark as an oracle and the Armenan oracle of Guido Von List. Such modern systems are based on traditional occultism such as Hermeticism and Cabala.

At the beginning of the 21st century, runes are rarely written as a script, except in Iceland. They survive on the edges of European society mainly used for fortune telling. In the modern runic oracle, the Futhark converts into the equivalent of the Tarot or the I Ching. Sets of runes can be bought ready made, incised in wood, stone and crystals by enthusiasts or cast in resin and plastic by manufacturers.

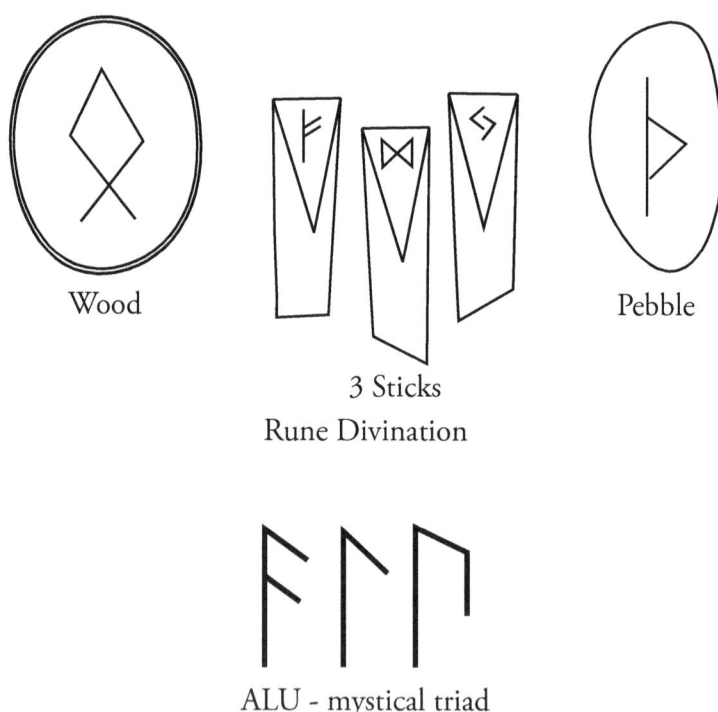

Wood   Pebble

3 Sticks
Rune Divination

ALU - mystical triad

Bind Runes

Bind Runes are letter symbols in which, one, two or more runes are bound together to form a magic sigil. The binding of letters that formed spells into mystical symbols was a popular practise throughout the Greek and Roman empire, and seems to have been continued by the Norse, using bind runes as charms and talismans for healing and protection.

Bind runes are true sigils as they are created with magic intent, whereas all runes and therefore all letters are considered magical by nature. Bind runes are sometimes mistakenly called Rune Staves. Rune Stave is the name given to a magic rune arrangement based around a single line or 'stave'. Stave is also the name given to runes arranged in a circular, radial or snowflake design. Such staves were used mainly on amulets for protection in battle and safety when travelling.

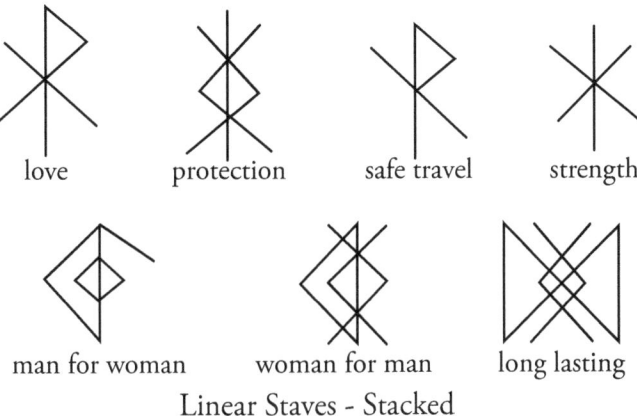

love   protection   safe travel   strength

man for woman   woman for man   long lasting

Linear Staves - Stacked

Same Stave Rune

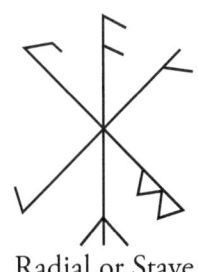

Radial or Stave

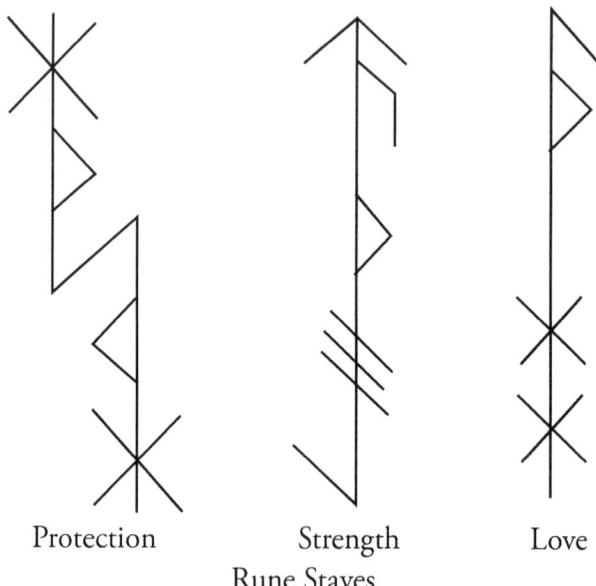

Protection   Strength   Love
Rune Staves

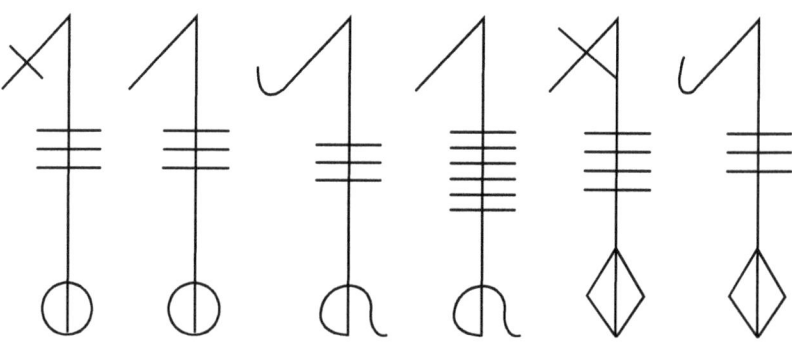

Sventhorn

Sventhorn are the most authentic of Viking symbols, mentioned many times in Nordic saga's including the saga of the Volsungr, the saga of King Hrolf Kraki and the saga of Gongu-Hrolf. Although their appearance, definition and magical qualities of the Sventhorn is somewhat different in every myth, they do have one thing in common. In all the stories, Sventhorn were used by Norse Gods and their people to put their adversaries into a deep, long sleep.

Galdrastafir

The most intricate of rune systems are the 17th century Icelandic staves called Galdrastafir, a mixture of Viking and Christian magic. It is the name given to the hundreds of Icelandic magical rune staves that appeared between 1400 and 1800, most from the 1600s. They are found in 17th century 'black' grimoires like the Huld manuscript. Some intermix Christian and Viking elements, others are solely Christian related.

It is likely that Galdrastafir appeared in Iceland after other symbols were seen in Medieval grimoires from mainland Europe, most likely influenced by the Keys of Solomon, as they contain sigils to banish demons and such.

Since the 1800s, Galdrastafir have been drawn and redrawn, many are missing or with added elements that change how the original looked. They were revived in the 19th century by the Geatish Society and re-revived as symbols associated with the Scandinavian Heathenism called Asatru in the 1970s and 80s

Although they do not originate from the Viking age they are steeped in Norse mythology and folklore, connected to the gods and goddesses and runic characters going back centuries.

Icelandic runes can be seen as a graphic representation of a magic spell or incantation, whose purpose can range from acquiring good fortune and protection in life to more sinister spells for raising the dead, causing ill health and even death. Spells conducted with Galdrastafir are known as Seioir and its male practitioners are called Seiomenn and its female ones Visendakona. Most of the time, their sorcery consists of white magic, designed for personal aid and the benefit of others. After carving the spells, they need to be activated by anointing the symbols with blood.

Galdrastafir can be divided into two separate forms, asymmetrical which are the older forms, created using the common method of sigil work for names and magic, and the symmetrical later forms which have a greater esotericism and range, from the most simple to the very complex and elaborate forms. There are different types of stave such as the Linear and radial as well as cartwheel formation, typically they make a snowflake shape. Elements include modifiers, runes drawn over the body of staves.

PAGAN SIGILS

14th century Greek variants of Solomonic seals

PAGAN SIGILS

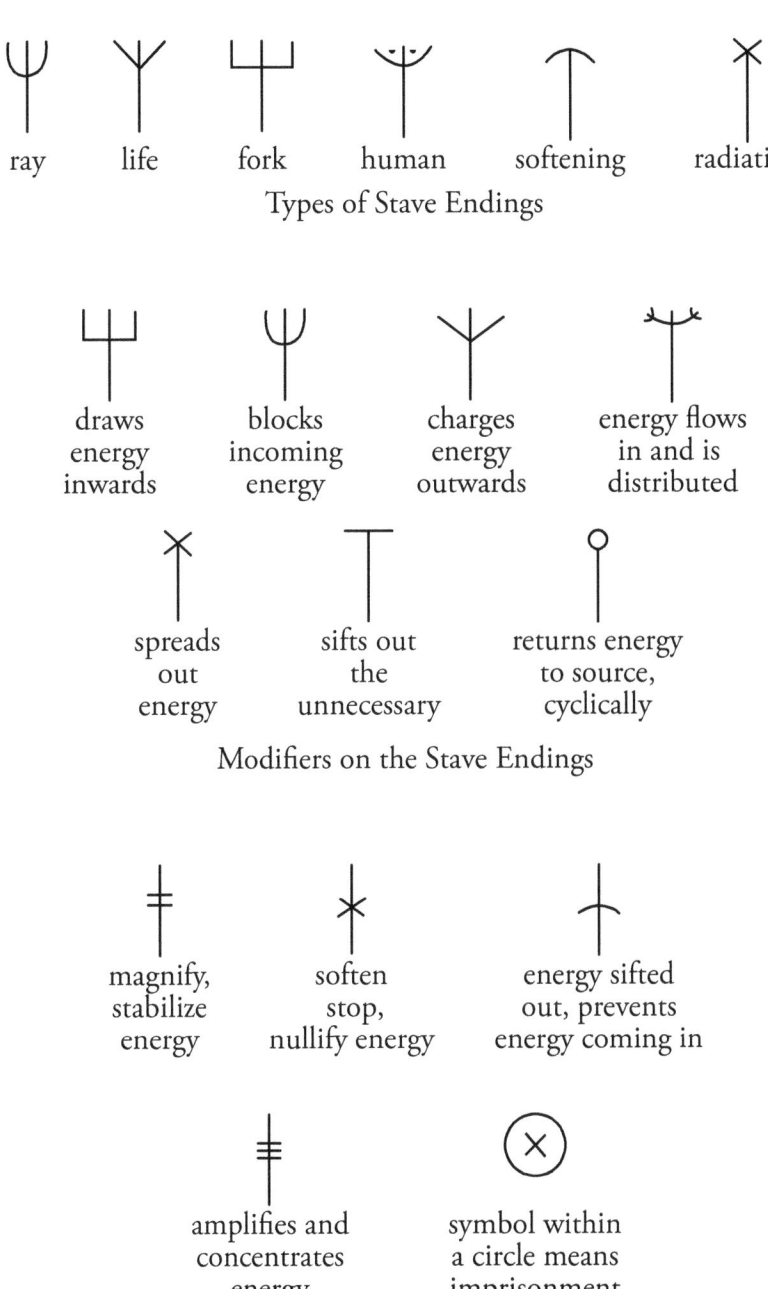

ray	life	fork	human	softening	radiating

Types of Stave Endings

draws energy inwards	blocks incoming energy	charges energy outwards	energy flows in and is distributed

spreads out energy	sifts out the unnecessary	returns energy to source, cyclically

Modifiers on the Stave Endings

magnify, stabilize energy	soften stop, nullify energy	energy sifted out, prevents energy coming in

amplifies and concentrates energy	symbol within a circle means imprisonment

Modifiers on the Stave Body

PAGAN SIGILS

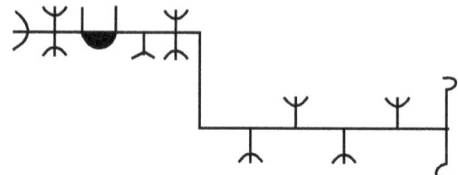

Feingur

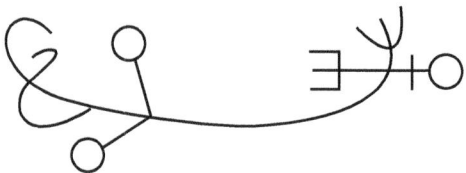

Ottastafur

   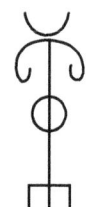

Theckur   Thrumur

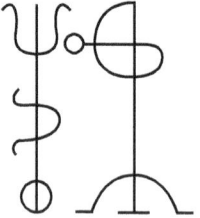   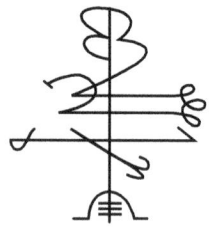

Drumstafir   Lukkustafir

Asymmetrical Staves

PAGAN SIGILS

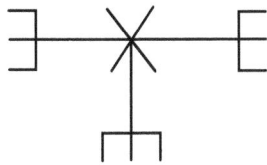

Ao unni
to get a girl

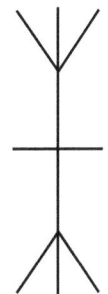

Donderbezen
Thunder Broom
protection against
lightning and
evil spirits

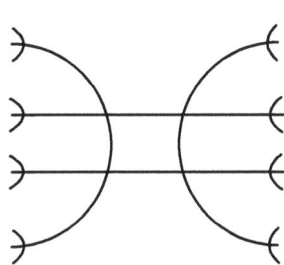

Gapaldur
ensures victory
in wrestling bouts

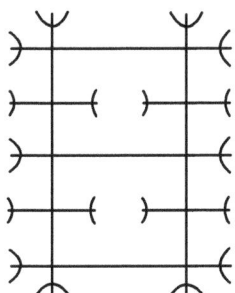

Brinsustafir
whetstone sigil

Symmetrical Staves

PAGAN SIGILS

Hugr - bird rune

Donder Kross - Thunder Cross

Ginfaxi - protection in battle

Ginnir - Divine, demonical

Aegishjalmur - protection in battle

Vegvisir - runic compass

Symmetrical Radial Staves (cartwheel)

Viedistafur - luck with fishing

Veldismagan - to increase power

Aegshjalmur - Seal of Moses
Snowflake Staves

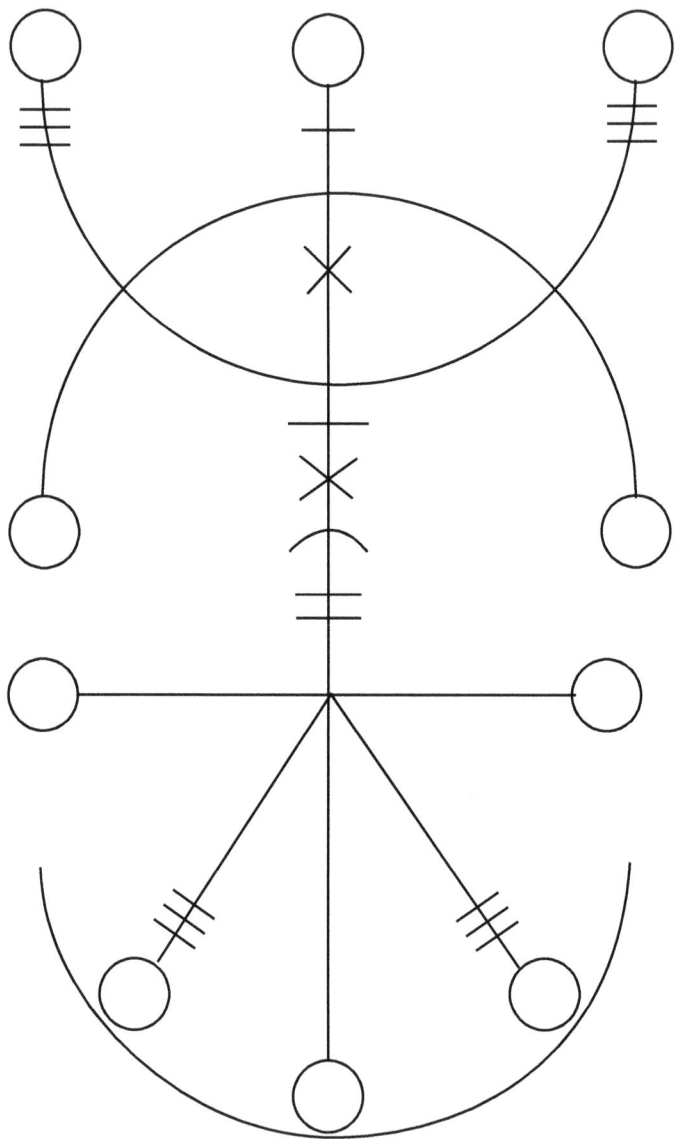

Nabrokarstatur
Stave for making trousers from dead man's skin, capable of producing an endless supply of money.

PAGAN SIGILS

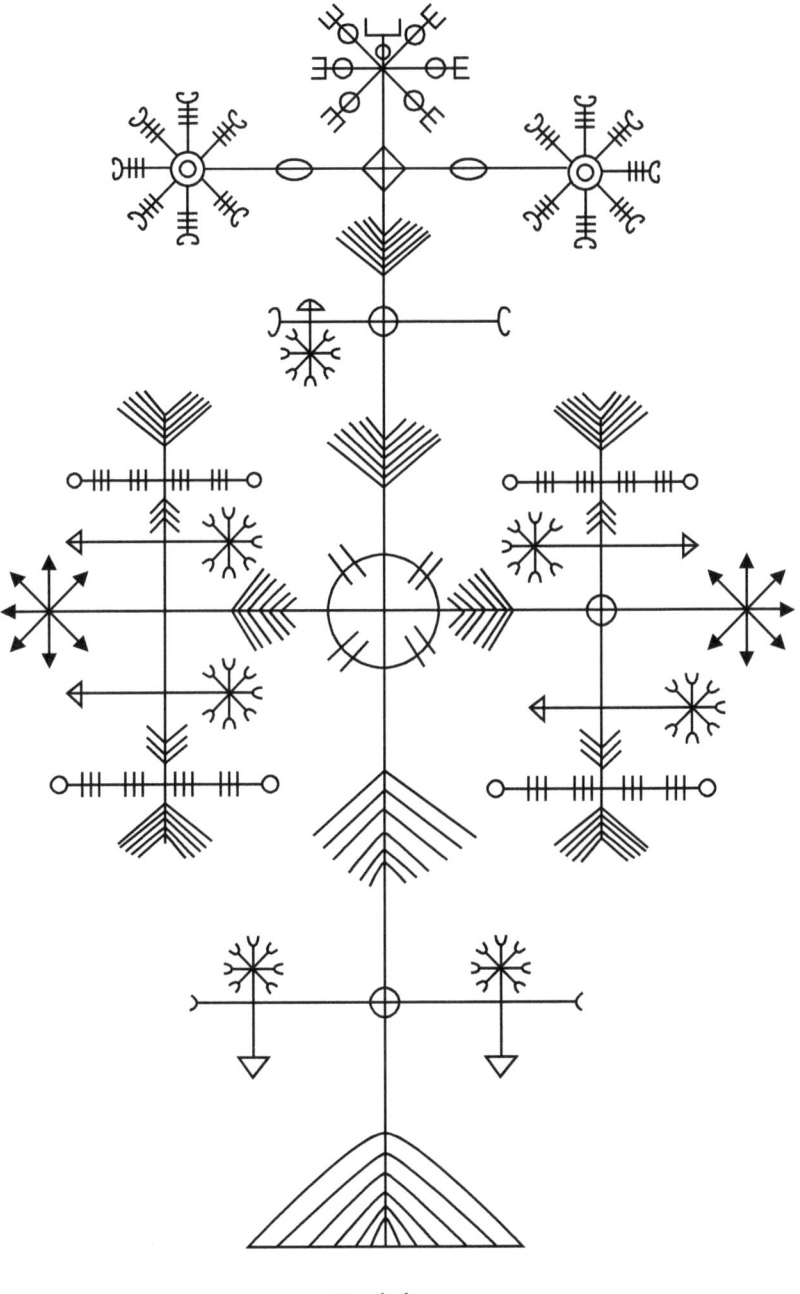

Rudukross

Runic Futhark

'Runic' meaning 'scratched' or 'carved', denotes a symbol system in which simple marks were added to a vertical line to create the individual staves used as an oracle for divination, calender making, and empowering amulets and talismans, before they became a systemized alphabet and script.

The origins of the runes lie the archaic pictographic symbolism linked to divination practices in sun, tree and fertility cults. These signs are found scratched in to rock, particularly at Hallristningar in Sweden, dating from before the end of the second bronze age, 1300 BC. These symbols are known as Ur-Runes (Urrunen), which refers to runes before they became systemized into a writing system or alphabet.

Around 500 BCE, the Roman derived Latin alphabet crossed the Alps from Italy into Germany, where the Drottir or Druids converted their goddess orientated, lunar based, tree calender into a runic alphabet and script. Over the next 500 years, the Germanic peoples of central and northwestern Europe created three national variants of the Futhark.

First, the German Elder Futhark (oldest alphabet) circa 500 BCE. Followed by the Anglo-Saxon Futhorc of Britain in the 6th century CE. Use of the Germanic Futhark came to an end in the early 9th century, replaced by the Latin alphabet of Christianity.

By 850 CE, the Younger Futhark, an entirely Scandinavian rune-row came into being and remained in use until the 16th century in Gotland. The last recorded use of the Futhark as a writing system was in 17th century Iceland.

The Younger Futhark was first documented in 17th Sweden. The Iron Age and Medieval variants of the Futhark were rediscovered and revived during the 18th, 19th and 20th century.

A secret form of Germanic runes are Kvistrunir or Branching runes, used as a cipher for encoding secret texts. Similar to Ogham runes in form, they have lines that flow upwards and downwards from either side of a stave in meaningful arrangements. Traditionally, the lines on the right stand for the position of the individual letter and the left line represents the number of the row it appears in.

PAGAN SIGILS

Ur-Runes (Urrunen) 1300 BCE

PAGAN SIGILS

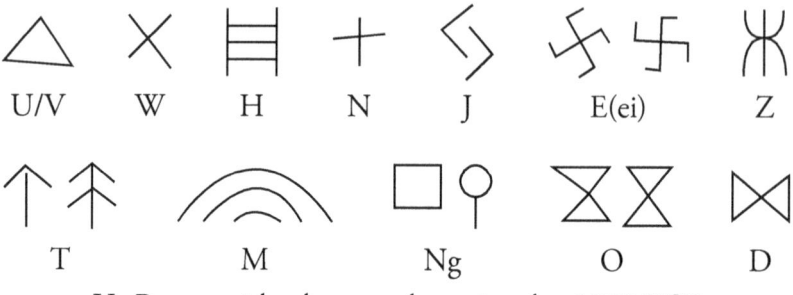

Ur-Runen with a known phonetic value 1200 BCE

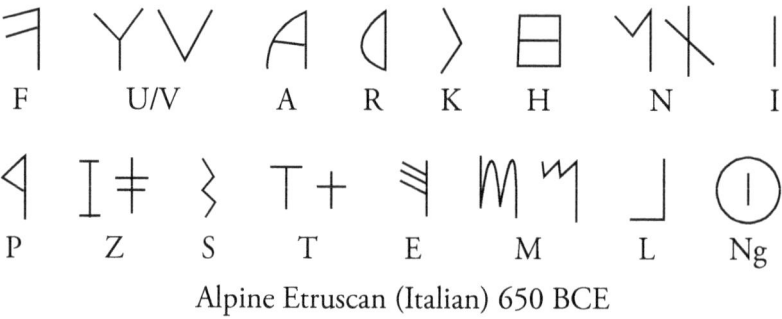

Alpine Etruscan (Italian) 650 BCE

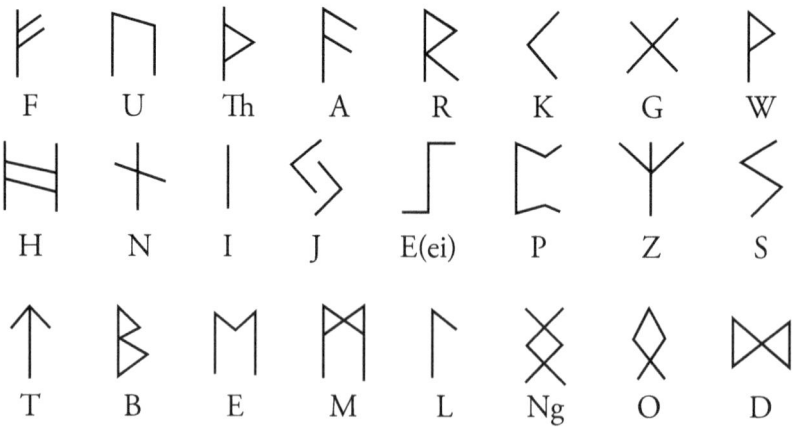

Germanic, Common, Elder Futhark 500 BCE

PAGAN SIGILS

Anglo-Saxon Futhorc 500 CE

Norse or Younger Futhark 850 CE

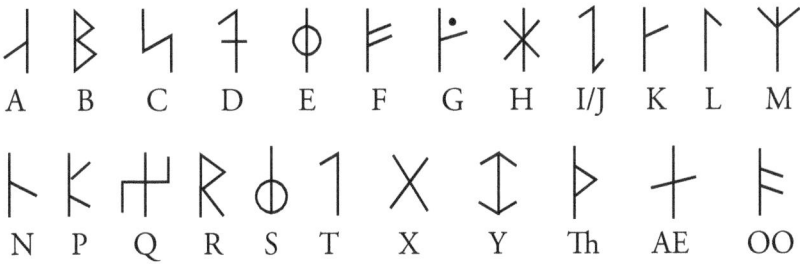

Icelandic 'Latin' runic alphabet 1970

PAGAN SIGILS

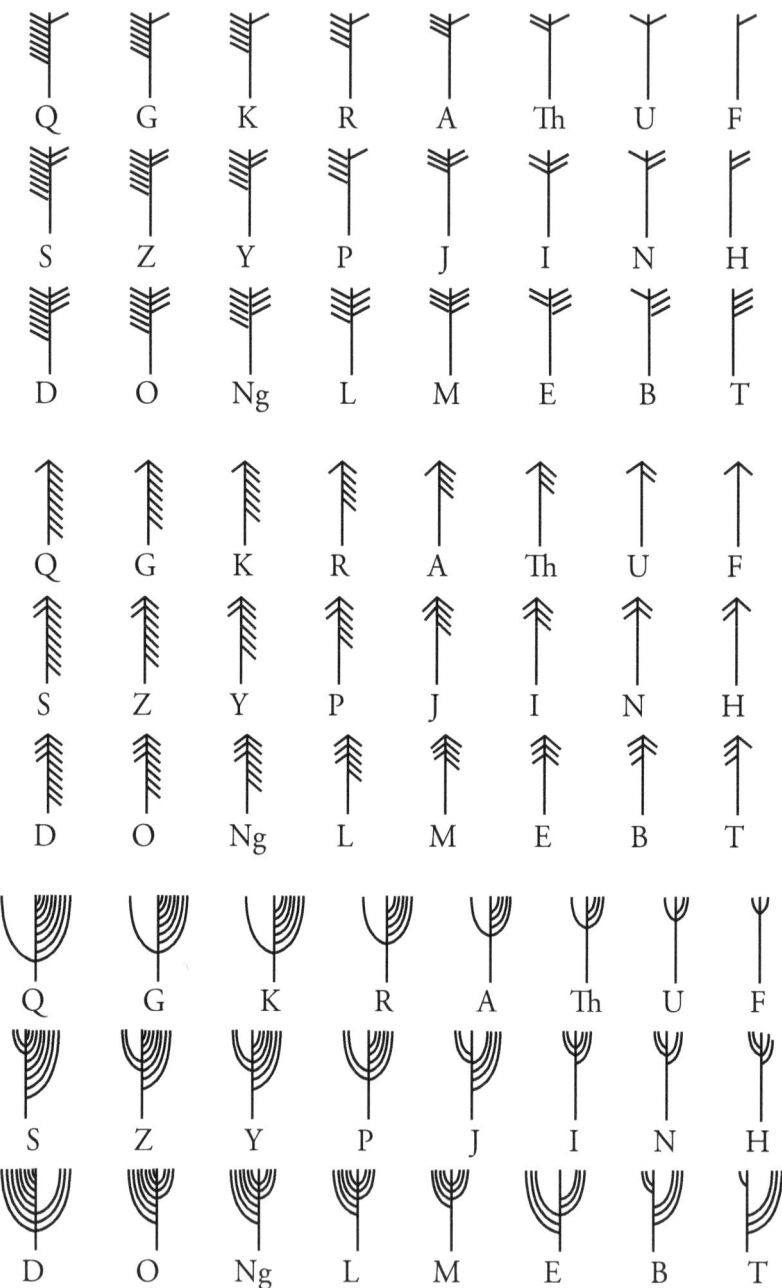

Kvistrumir - Branching rune ciphers

Runic Oracle

Following hundreds of years of neglect, 20th century Germanic occultists revived the Elder Futhark as an oracle. In this oracle system, the runes represent the forces of nature and mind from which one seeks advice.

The origins of the runic oracle is found in the Odinic Mysteries. In Norse mythology, everything that exists is connected in a vast web called the Web of the Wyrd or the Matrix of Fate, a construct of nine staves symmetrically arranged on an angular grid, woven by the Norns or Three Fates. On this web is situated Yggdrasil, the Cosmic Tree. Whilst hanging upside down on Yggdrasil, Odin took the nine staves of the Cosmic Law of Creation or the Web of the Wyrd and cast them to the ground, where they formed the patterns that revealed the 24 runes of the Elder Futhark to him.

Rune means 'a mystery' in Old Norse and each of the original 24 magical runes had a name, the initial letter of which represented its phonetic value, a symbolic image and esoteric meaning, as well as correspondences to trees denoting the months of the lunar year for calendar making. For divination purposes, the 24 runes were divided into 3 lots of 8 called families or aetirs, each assigned to a God - Freya's eight, Hegel's eight and Tyr's eight.

Runic Wheel
almanac, lunar/solar calender, sun dial, birth chart, etc.

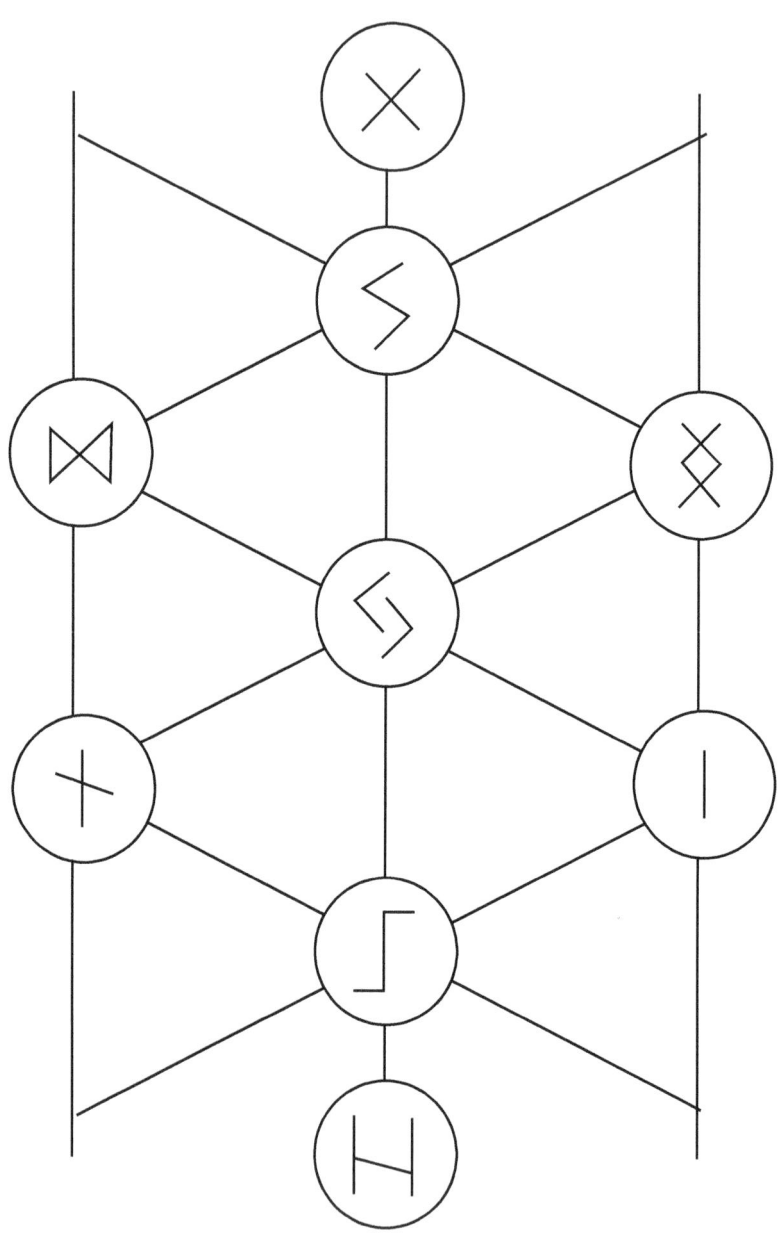

Web of the Wyrd and Ygdrassil

PAGAN SIGILS

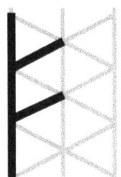

F - Feoh
elder
fire/earth
Freya.
movable wealth

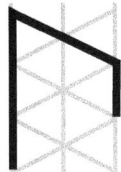

U - Ur
birch
earth
Thor
strength

Th - Thorn
oak
fire
Thor
attack/defense

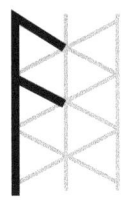

A - As
ash
air
Odin
primal sound

R - Rad
oak
air
Ing
travel, action

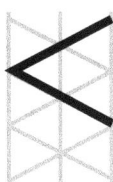

K - Ken
pine
fire
Heindall
torch, beacon

G - Gyfu
ash/elm
air
Gefn
gift, sacred mark

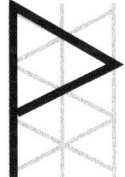

W - Wyn
ash
earth
Odin
joy, harmony

Freya's Aetir

PAGAN SIGILS

  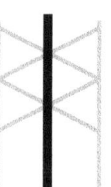

H - Hagal
ash/yew
ice
Urd
transformation

N - Nyd
beech/rowan
fire
Skuls
necessity

I - Is
alder
ice
Verdandi
icicle

 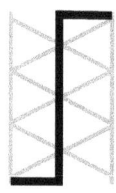 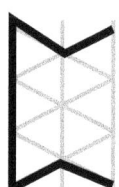

J - Jera
oak
earth
Freya
harvest

Y - Eoh
yew/poplar
all
Ullr
regeneration

P - Peorth
beech
water
Frigg
womb, fate

 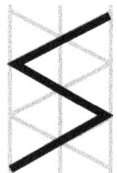

Z - Elhaz
yew
air
Heindall
defense

S - Sigel
juniper
air
balder
sun

Hagal's Aetir

PAGAN SIGILS

T - Tyr
oak
air
Tyr
justice

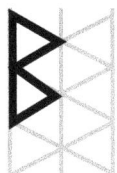

B - Beorc
birch
earth
Nerthus
growth

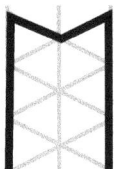

E - Ehwas
oak/ash
earth
Freya
intuitive bonds

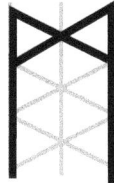

M - Manu
holly
air
Heindall
mankind

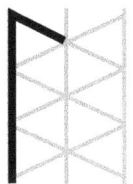

L - Lagu
osier
water
Njord
womb, sea

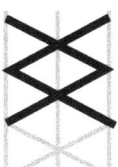

Ng - Ing
apple
water.earth
Ing
potential

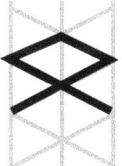

O - Odal
hawthorn
earth
Odin
land, property

D - Dag
spruce
fire/air
Heindall
balence

Tyr's Aetir

PAGAN SIGILS

Rune	Name	Tree	Element	Deity	Meaning
ᚪ	Ac	Oak	fire	Thor	potential
ᚩ	Os	Ash	air	Odin	speech
ᚣ	Ur	Yew	all	Odin/Frigg	bow
ᛡ	Iur	Ivy	water	Njord	world serpent
ᛠ	Ear	Yew	earth	Hela	death

4th Aetir

Rune	Name	Tree	Element	Deity	Meaning
ᛢ	Cweorth	bay/beech	fira	Loge	funeral pyre
ᛣ	Calc	maple	earth	Norns	grail
ᛥ	Stan	witch hazel	earth	Nerthus	sacred stone
ᚸ	Gar	ash/spindle	all	Odin	spear of Odin
	Wolfsangel	yew	earth	Vidar	wolf hook
	Ziu	oak	air/fire	Tyr	thunderbolt
	Erda	elder/birch	earth	Erda	Mother Earth
	Ul	blackthorn	air	Waldh	turning point
	Sol	juniper	fire	Sol	the Sun

5th Aetir

Anglo-Saxon addiitions

Modern Runic Oracle

The modern runic oracle originates in the 17th century when Swedish academic, Hermeticist and Rosicrucian Johnnes Bureus was the first to document runes and develop a runic system based on the Younger Futhark and Cabala, naming them Adulrunen or 'Noble runes' in 1611.

Also based on the Younger Futhark, the Armenan runes were revealed to Austrian esotericist Guido Von List in 1902. He published them in his text, Das Getheimnis der Runen, assigning specific meanings to each rune that vary greatly from the Elder Futhark.

They were employed for magical purposes in German mysticism before and after WW1, expanded and reformed by later rune masters including Karl Maria Wiligut, who was responsible for their adoption in to Nazi occultism, which is why Armenan runes are often referred to as Hitler runes

Werner Kosab's system combines modern runes with older forms, along with symbols derived from the Hermetic tradition to create his 56 sigil runic oracle.

From the 1980s onwards, several more modern systems of runic divination were published. The first of these books was written in 1980 by Ralph Blum. His system employs the runes of the Elder Futhark plus a blank, making 25, arranged in five rows of five.

Other systems also include a 'blank' rune, as a replacement for a lost rune. According to Blum it was Odin's rune, the rune of the beginning and the end, representing the 'divine' in all human transactions. Blum also pioneered the direct correlation between the runes and the Tarot cards with the inclusion of rune cards and 'spreads'. The runes are either selected one by one from a closed bag or thrown down at random for a reading.

Adulrunen (Noble runes) - Johames Burus 1611

PAGAN SIGILS

ᚠ F - Fa - generate your luck and you will have it

ᚢ U - Ur - know yourself, then you will know all

ᚦ Th - Thurs - preserve your ego

ᚨ A / O - Os - your spirit force makes you free

ᚱ R - Rit - I am right, this rod right is indestructable, therefore, I am indestructable

ᚲ K - Ka - your blood, your highest possession

ᚼ H - Hag - harbour the All in yourself and you will control the All

ᚾ N - Nor - use your fate, do not strive against it

ᛁ I - Is - win power over youself and you will have power over everything in the spiritual and physical world

ᛅ A - Ar - respect the primal fire

ᛌ S Sig - the creative spirit must conquer

ᛏ T - Tyr - fear not death, it cannot kill you

ᛒ B - Bar - the life strands in the hands of God, trust it in you

PAGAN SIGILS

⌐ L - Laf - first learn to steer, then do the sea journey

Ψ M - Man - be a man

⅄ Y - Yr - think about the end

⟊ E - Em - marriage is the raw-root of the Aryan

⋈ G - Gibor - Man, be one with God

Armenan runes (Aryan cabala) Von List 1902

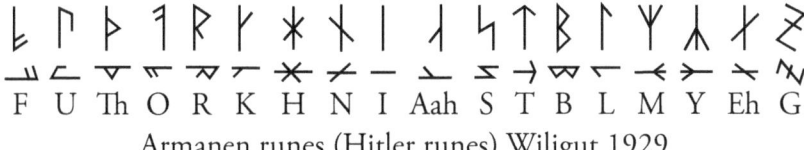

F U Th O R K H N I Aah S T B L M Y Eh G

Armanen runes (Hitler runes) Wiligut 1929
horizontal and vertical variants

"Das Runen Orikal" Werner Kosab

PAGAN SIGILS

5. U Uruz Strength	4. O Othila Separation	3. A Anuz Signals	2. G Gebo Partnership	1. M Mammaz Self
10. Z Algiz Protection	9. E(ei) Eihwaz Defence	8. Ng Inguz Fertility	7. N Nauthiz Constraint	6. P Perth Initiation
15. T Teiwaz Warrior	14. K Kono Opening	13. J Jera Harvest	12. W Wunjo Joy	11. F Fehu Possessions
20. R Raido Journey	19. H Hagalz Disruption	18. L Laguz Flow	17. E Ehwaz Movement	16. B Berkana Growth
25. Blank rune Odin Unknowable	24. S Sowelu Wholeness	23. I Isa Standstill	22. D Dagaz Breakthrough	21. Th Thinisa Gateway

Viking Runic Oracle of Robert Blum

Slavic Heathenism (Rodnov)

Since the early 20th century there has been a reinvention and reinstituationalisation of Slavic religion by the Rodnov or 'native faith' movement. Rodnovery, Rodnover, Rodnoverie or Rodzimowiers is practised throughout Eastern Europe with groups in Russia, Ukraine, Belarus, Lithuania, Latvia, Estonia, Finland, Poland, Hungary, Czech republic, Slovakia, Bulgaria, Serbia, Bosnia-Herzegovina and Armenia.

Most Rodnov groups are as recent as the 1990s with more still forming in the early 21st century. The forbears of Rodnovery are to be found in 18th century Slavic Romanticism which glorified the pre Christian beliefs of the Slavs. In the 1930s and 40s, practitioners established groups in Poland and Ukraine

Rodnov draws from ancient Slavic folk religion, often combining it with philosophical underpinnings taken from other religions, mainly elements of Vedism, as it is believed that the Slavic Gods are the same as the Vedic Gods. Some groups adapt Iranian (Aryan) religions such as Avestanism and Zoroastrianism.

Rodnov is Wiccan in origin but differs from Wicca in that it is reconstructed paganism, unlike Wicca which is eclectic paganism. Some Rodnov groups focus almost exclusively on folk religion and the worship of the gods at the right times of year. While others have developed a scriptural core, represented by writings purported to be centuries old documents such as the Book of Veles, writings which elaborate powerful national mythologemes such as the Mira of Sylenkoism and esoteric writings such as the Slavo-Aryan Vedas of Yinglism.

Founded in 1992, the Ancient Russian Yinglist Church of the Orthodox Old Believers is a Russian neopagan religion classified as a branch of Rodnov, but not often recognized as such by mainstream Rodnov groups. Yingly is the primordial fiery force from which the Universe has risen.

Yinglists also worship Rod similarly to other Rodnov groups, but consider it the archetypical God of Embodiment and the God of the Begotten (manifested) World.

Rod - Kolovrat

As the symbol of the original Supreme God Rod, the Kolovrat is a symbol of spiritual and secular power and as such, it is the pan Slavic symbol of Rodnov.

'Kolo' mean 'wheel; and 'vrat' means 'spokes', each turn of the wheel is a cycle of life in our world, symbolizing the endless cycle of births and deaths, sun and fire, strength and dignity. It symbolizes Rod, who created the world and all that exists wirhin it. He also seperated the material world from the spiritual world.

Veles

Veles or Weles is the Slavic God of the Underworld, the keeper of all thresholds and ruler of the world. He is the Horned God of Slavic paganism, god of all animals, wealth, abundance and magic.

Perun

Perun is the God of Thunder and Lightning, a supreme deity of the Slavic peoples. Everything that has ever been struck by thunder, especially Oak trees were marked with the Perunika or Thundermark, a symbol denoting the sacred. The Thundermark was also found painted onto the roofs of buildings to protect them form thunder and lightning.

Dazbog

Dazbog, spelt in many different variations, is the God of the sun, happiness, destiny and justice, who later became a Supreme deity. As the Son of Svarog, he rode across the sky in a golden chariot pulled by four fire breathing lions and is associated with Mithra, Helios and Satan.

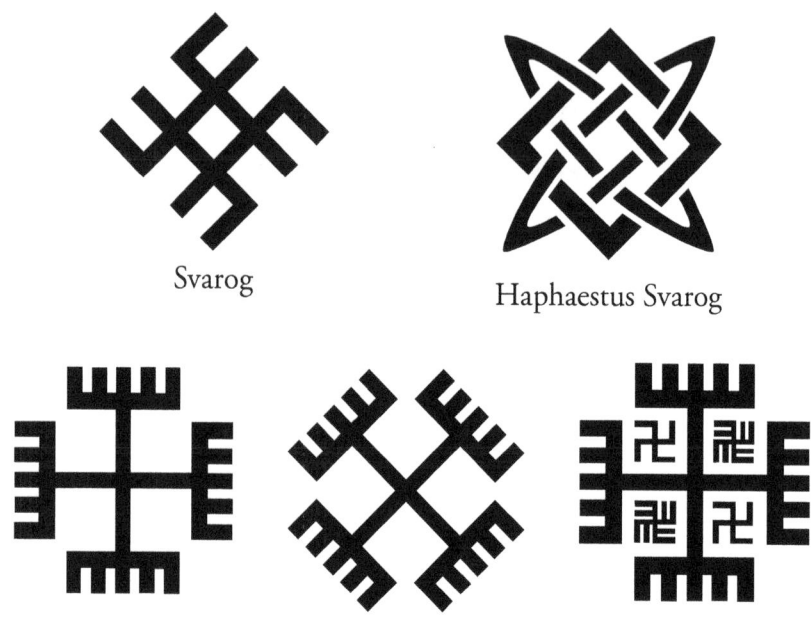

Svarog

Haphaestus Svarog

Hands of Svarog

Svarog

While most Slavs use the name Rod to invoke God, others use Nebo (Heaven) or Svarog. Svarog is one of a trinity of Slavic deities along with Perum and Dazbog, who mirror the Trimurti of Vedic Gods, Brahma, Vishnu and Shiva.

The Supreme and Heavenly God in Slavic religion, Svarog is a god of fire, sun, heaven and virility. His name id derived from the same root as those of 'qyarrel' and 'dispute'. He is the guardian of the sacred fire and associated by name, Haphaestus Svarog, with blacksmiths and forging iron, he formed all the other gods from his sparks. He is also known by the name Zuarasici.

Svarog is popular amongst Rodnov groups and takes three forms. The sigil called the Hands of Svarog or Hands of God, recalls how Svarog created the world using his hands, not by using magic. The sigil represents Heaven and the all powerful Svarog. The two forms of swastika in the interior represent the sun which gives life to those on Earth.

Auseklis Belobog

Gods of Light

The symbol of the male God Auaeklis is a representation of light defeating dark. It is seen as a rising sun, rising star or rising moon. A symbol for the protection of men. Beloog is the White God of luck, light, happiness, fortune and a plentiful harvest, a symbol of wealth and a protection.

Mokosh Lada

Goddesses

Sometimes called the Great Mother, Mokosh is a Goddess of female endevours such as spinning, weaving and shearing. She is often invoked to protect women in child birth and is associated with destiny and fate, especially of women.

Lada is the goddess of beauty and fertitliy. Her symbol or star serves to protect against negative energy or dark forces. The circle represents the sun, the four points represent faith, freedom, righteousness and honour.

PAGAN SIGILS

AKA
Double Cross
Sun & Energy
Unity & World Order
Water Well
start of agricultural year

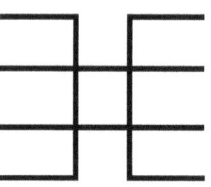

DZIVIBA
Light
New Beginnings
Life Journey
Strength
Protection

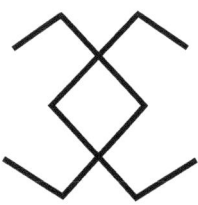

KRUPTIS
The Subconscious
Intuition
Knowledge
Wisdom
Strength

AUSTRA'S TREE
World Order
Past, Present, Future
Beautiful & Valuable
Blessings
Success

ZALKTIS
Snake
The Changeable
Wisdom & Knowledge
Life Energy,
Communication

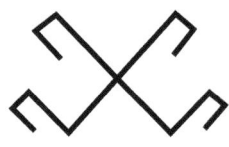

MARTINS
Embellishment of Jurnis
Productivity
Fertility
Prosperity

Latvian Runes

Svarga
A cosmogram showing how God organized the heavens around Polaris, the celestial north pole star This view of the organization of the heavens dates back to at least Neolithic times.

Rantha
The name of God in stylized Yinglist runes.

Ynglist symbols

British Neopaganism

The Neopagan movement in Britain is primarily represented by witchcraft and Wicca religions, Druidry and Heathenism, plus various Satanic, Shamanic and New Age groups.

British Neopaganism begins in the 18th century with the Age of Enlightenment, whose logic inspired a fading of belief in witchcraft, leading to the publication of the 1760 Witchcraft Act in England. In the same century, the Romantic movement saw a renewed interest in ancient British and Celtic art, literature and religion.

This continued throughout the 19th century, as paganism came to the attention of British occultists through various international events and cultural developments, including fresh archeological discoveries in Egypt, a growing interest in Egyptian history and the formation of the Folklore Society in 1878.

The late Victorian Celtic renaissance inspired authors, artists, philosophers, scientists and lay people to increasingly turn to Celtic, Egyptian, Greco-Roman, Eastern and other forms of paganism for inspiration and values that were not driven by contemporary industrialism and materialism. By the early 20th century, there were established Heathen brotherhoods, Druid groves and Witches covens across Britain.

Europe produced many notable societies and occultists who blended popular interest in spiritualism with Romantic notions of the contemporary relevance of early Egyptian, Greek and Eastern religions and symbolism. The most influential of these groups was the Hermetic Order of the Golden Dawn which included British occultist Aleister Crowley in its membership. Crowley went on to be become the most influential and infamous figure to come out of the early 20th century occult scene.

In 1945, Robert Graves published his influential book 'The White Goddess', in which Celtic mythologies are reconstructed. The repeal of the Witchcraft Act in 1951 allowed Gerald Gardner to publish Witchcraft Today in 1954, laying the foundation stone of Wicca. This situation gave rise not only to Wicca and Neo-Druidism, but also to Goddess worship, Earth religions, Neoshamanism, New Age movements, Luciferianism and Satanism, all predominantly British in origin.

Celtic Knots

Celtic knots are stylized graphic representations of knots used in decoration such as the braiding and of plaiting hair, that were adapted into the ornamentation of Christian monuments and manuscripts such as the Book of Kells. The use of these interlaced patterns has its origins in the late Roman empire.

Knot patterns appear between the 2nd and 4th centuries CE in Roman floor mosaics. Such patterns are also found in Byzantine, Coptic, Ethiopian and Islamic culture, as well as Celtic art. There are eight basic variations, Trinity, Spiral, Sailors, Dara, Shield, Cross, Solomon and Celtic knots.

Triqueta

A Trinity knot with three interlocking pieces that represent where the three circles would overlap. Used to represent the Christian Trinity, it was a Celtic symbol of feminine spirituality, as in the Triple Goddess or mind, body spirit. In Heathenism, it is associated with Odin, through the Valknut symbol. Occasionally, the Triqueta appears within a circle, intersected with a triangle.

Triskelion

This spiral knot or triple spiral symbol is typically considered a Celtic design but it is also found in Buddhist writings. Throughout history it has appeared in a variety of forms and places including ancient Lycae, Mycenae, Sicily and the Isle of Man. It represents the power of three, in the case of the Celts this meant earth, sky, and sea.

British Neopagan Scripts

Neopagan scripts fall into two categories, those that have been revived from the past and those new scripts based on pagan symbolism with no occult or literary history.

The Biobel Loath script was revived by the 19th century Celtic Romantics. Of all the British neopagan scripts, the most authentic are the Barddas or Bardic runes, used to write the Welsh druidic text called The Barddas.

Pecti Wita is the modern revival name for Scottish or ancient Pictish paganism. The Pecti Wita rune script has no antiquity and is used mainly for fortune telling. The Pictish swirl script is said to be part of the ancient Pictish writing system, although it is thought that the ancient Picts employed no alphabetic writing system. As a cipher for the English alphabet it is inspired by the spiral patterns found on ancient Pictish stonework and is used for spell casting. Horizontal Branching Ogham script is also a modern invention.

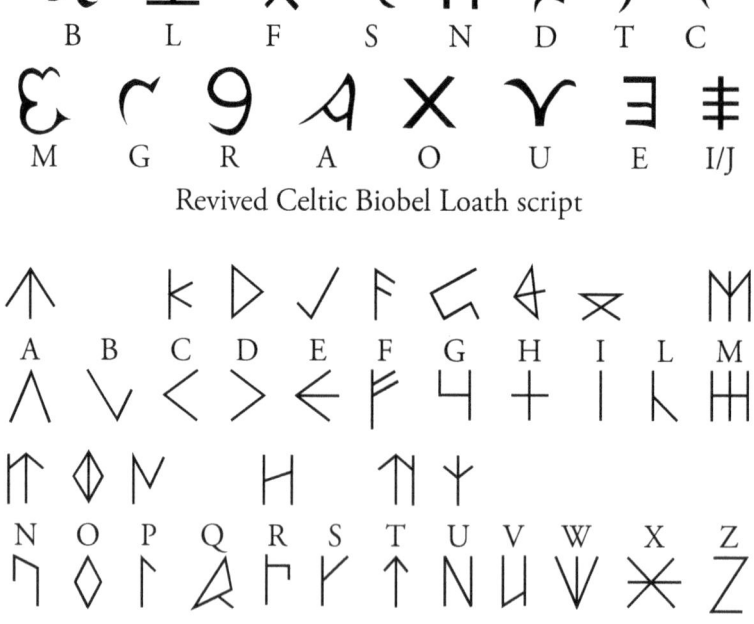

Revived Celtic Biobel Loath script

Bardic or Barddas runes

PAGAN SIGILS

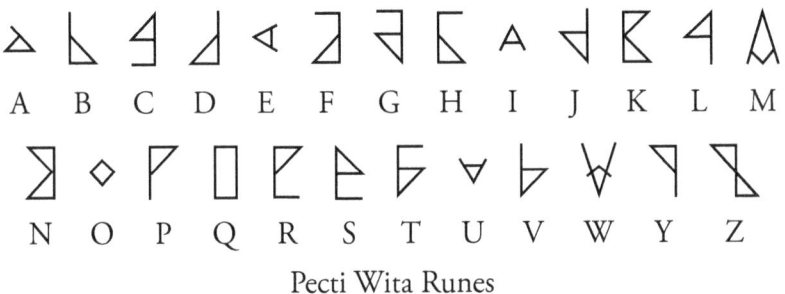

Pecti Wita Runes

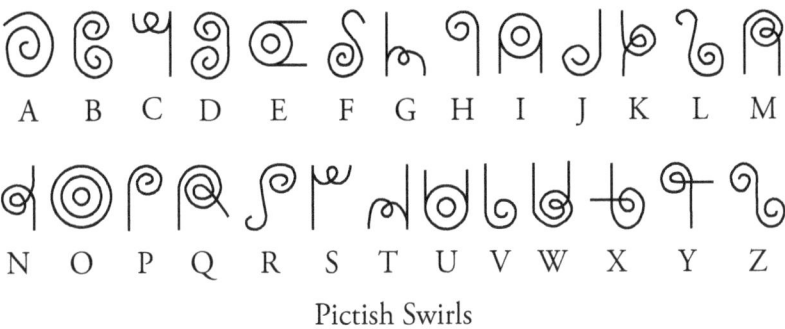

Pictish Swirls

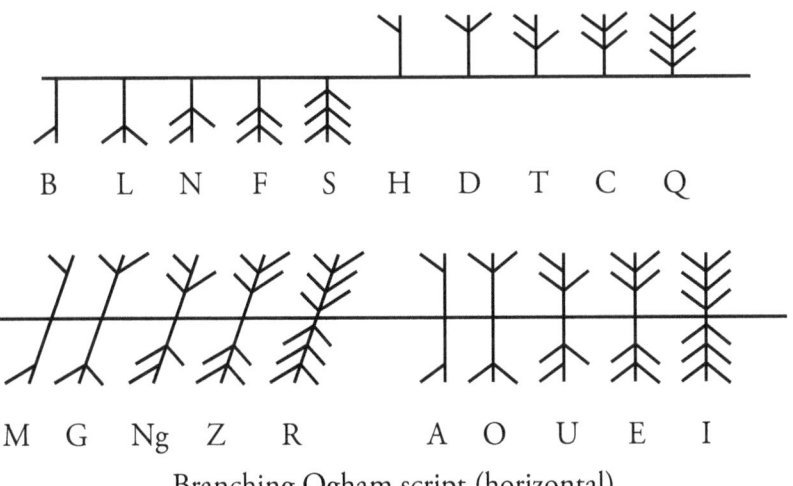

Branching Ogham script (horizontal)

British Heathenism

British Heathenism begins with the first flourishing of Anglo-Saxon studies in the 17th and 18th centuries. Today, it is primarily present in two forms. Odinism, an international German movement, and Anglo-Saxon heathenism, Esetroth or Fyrnsiou meaning 'ancient custom' in Old English. Both forms of British heathenry draw from the Anglo-Saxon identity and culture of England, with almost no difference between them.

The Odinic Rite was founded in England in 1973 and in 1988 became the first polytheistic religion to be awarded Registered Charity status. In 2021, Asatru UK had almost 3000 Facebook members.

Community sigil for the
Anglo-Saxon pagan temple at Yeavering

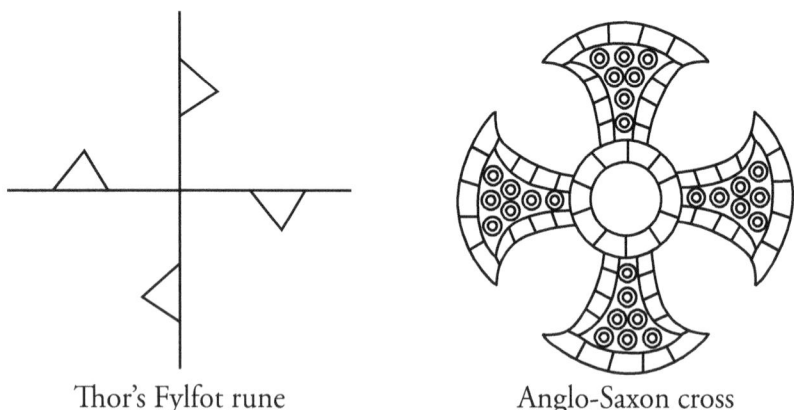

Thor's Fylfot rune   Anglo-Saxon cross

Neo Druidism

Neo Druidism is a modern spiritual movement that generally promotes harmony, connection and reverence for the natural world. Although most of the early druids identified as Christian, many modern forms of druidry are neopagan religions. Neo Druidism has it roots in the 18th century Romantic movement of the Rhine land, in Switzerland and Austria, home of the ancestral Iron Age Celtic 'La Terne' culture, as well as Ireland and Britain.

Druid is the English translation of the Irish-Gaelic 'Doire' meaning 'Oak tree' symbolizing 'Wisdom'. They were members of a high ranking class in Celtic culture. Druids observed the lunar and solar year, its seasonal cycles and eight Holy days including Yule. Their places of worship were clearings in woods or forests and in timber and stone circles such as Stonehenge. In the fist century CE, Emperor Tiberius banned Druidism because of its supposed human sacrifices. After the second century, Druidism appears to have ended, probably sent into decline by the arrival of Christianity.

During the Iron Age, Celtic polytheism was the predominant religion in the area now known as England. Modern British Druidism has its roots in the Celtic revival of 18th century Romanticism. Its first organized group was the Ancient Order of Druids and included the artist and Arch Druid William Blake. Founded in London 1781 along Masonic lines, it is not considered neopagan. It was followed in 1792 by the Gorsedd of Bards of the Isle of Britain. Its rituals form an important part of the Welsh national Eisteddford. It's members include British royalty and senior clergy and is not considered to be a neopagan institution.

At the beginning of the 20th century, George Watson and MacGregor Reid began promoting Druidism as a spiritual path that could unite followers of many different faiths. Called the Universal Bond, they became a vehicle for conveying the ideas of the Theosophical Society and the Golden Dawn.

In the 1940s and 50s, the Universal Bond evolved in to the Ancient Druid Order, becoming the first such organization to be considered neopagan, being influenced by the occult movements of the 18th century. It attracted the catalystic figures of Gerald Gardner and Ross Nichols. Gardner become a seminal figure in Wicca. Nichols developed Druidism, focusing on Celtic lore and mythology. Both men were influenced by Robert Grave's The White Goddess.

The Order of Bards, Ovates and Druids split from the Ancient Druids Order in 1964 and began to deliver a more neopagan style of Druidry influenced by Wicca. By 1969, Druids were starting to appear in the ever growing Counter Culture, thanks to John Lennon's realization that Peace and Love, as the cornerstone of counter culture revolution connected with Druidism. More overtly Neopagan Druid groups developed in Britain from the 1970s onwards, including the British Druid Order and the Druid Network.

There are many similarities between Druidism and Wicca. Both emphasize the importance of developing a close link with nature. Both stress the importance of guardianship of the Earth and environmentalism. Some distinctions are that Druidism is more purely Celtic than Wicca. There is less emphasis on magic in Druidry and Druidry more actively encourages the development of music and poetry as paths to spiritual growth.

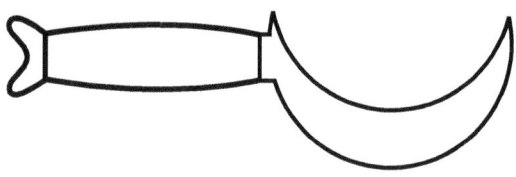

Boline

A knife in the Druid and Wiccan tradition. Its specific symbolism is in its blade, which shaped like the crescent moon and silver in colour. It usually has a white handle, also a reference to the moon.

It is a practical ceremonial tool often used for cutting herbs and in the case of Druids, they use it for cutting mistletoe directly from the tree.

Awen (OBOD)

Awen is the Welsh word for 'inspiration' or 'essence' and can be intoned in the same way as Om/Aum and used as a meditative focus. Developed by Lollo Morganwg in the late 1700s, it represents the divine rays of the triad, past, present and future, love, truth and knowledge, etc, Modern variants include three drops over the rays representing the three drops that imparted Gwion Bach with great wisdom.

Founded in England 1964, as a split from the Ancient Druid Order, the Order of Bards, Ovates and Druids placed the three lines and dots within three concentric rings, further amplifying the meaning, placing it in a protective circle.

RDNA

The Reform Druids of North America formed in 1963, Corteton Collage, Northfields, Minnesota as a protest against the colleges required attendance of religious services.

There are now over 40 groves and proto-groves across the USA and Canada. The popular generic meaning of the symbol is for Earth Mother and fertility.

Sigil of the Cosmos

Depicted on clergy vestments used by the American Druid Federation. The sigil of the cosmos is a microcosm of the universe depicting concepts sacred to ancient Indo-Europeans.

The top third is the realm of the sky, sun, moon, and celestial deities. The middle third is the realm of land, four corners of the world, earth deities, nature spirits, sacred hearth at its center, The bottom third is the realm of the sea, sacred wells, ancestors, underworld and chthonic deities. The Triple Realm symbols are aligned on the Axis Mundi or World Tree.

Tree Ogham

Pronounced, Oh-m or Oh-wam, meaning 'language' or 'eloquence', Ogham is an ancient Celtic writing system, named after Oghma, the Celtic God of poetry and eloquence.

As a script style, it is thought to be graphically derived from Tree Ogham, one of many Ogham systems employed by the Druids. All of which could be communicated using Ogham sign language, in which different finger signs are stroked along the ridge of the nose or shin to communicate. As most Ogham systems were number ciphers this may account for Ogham scripts resemblance to tally marks.

Originally an alphabet of 20 letters, it was increased to 25 with the addition of 5 extra letters to write Greek words in Irish. The known magical use of Ogham is limited to that of a lunar and solar calendar, divination, fortune telling, writing curses and charms.

The use of Ogham script died out around 500 AD, when it was replaced by the Roman letters of the Latin alphabet. It was revived by the neopaganist movement of the 20th century.

The tally arrays of Ogham script represents the sounds of Celtic language by using a series of ordered lines or branches, that emanate from either side or across a central line or trunk to form individual letters called Fews.

In the Tree Ogham alphabet, the 20 Fews are set out into 4 sets of 5 letters called 'groves' that represent the seasons. The Fews represent the months, the equinoxes and solstices of the lunar and solar calender.

Occultly, Tree Ogham differs from cabala, in that cabala has one tree, whereas Ogham has 'groves' filled with many trees and woodland plants.

As a divination system, Ogham Fews are carved into slivers of wood and thrown on to a cloth where the spread is interpreted. Historically, they were incised on four yew wands.

The questioner must take a minimum of 3 staves from the bag and cast them on the floor. The closest represent the past. The ones in the middle show the present and those furthest away reveal the future.

In Celtic mysticism, Tree Ogham employs the initial letter of the names of trees arranged in sequential order for calendar making.

This practice was common in the bronze age, employed from Palestine to Ireland and universally associated with the Triple Moon Goddess of the 3 season lunar year, before it was adapted to act as the 4 season, solar calendar of the Sun God.

The origin of this botanical system has its roots in the seasonal plants, shrubs and trees found in the Rhine land of Switzerland and Austria, home of the ancestral Iron Age Celtic 'La Terne' culture.

The Celts believed that humans were descended from trees. Because of this, trees played an important role in their religious beliefs.

Celtic Druids were said to be able to manipulate the alphabet to create sounds that brought about creation or manifestation. These sounds were correlated by bards - druids who specialised in music, to correspond to musical notes which were said to insight inanimate objects at the druid's will.

Tree Ogham Alphabet
(BLN variant)

Letter	Ogham	Irish	English	Date
AA		Palm	Palm	NY Day
A		Alim	Silver Fir	New Year
O		Onn	Gorse/Furze	Spr. eqx
U		Ura	Heather	Sum. sols
E		Eadha	White Poplar	Aut. eqx
I		Idhu	Yew	Win. sols
II, J, Y			Mistletoe	Dec 23

Vowels

Letter	Ogham	Irish	English	Date
B		Beth	Birch	Dec 25
L		Luis	Rowan	Jan 21
N		Nion	Ash	Feb 18
F(V)		Fearn	Alder	March 18
S		Saile	Willow	April 15

Letter	Ogham	Irish	English	Date
H		Uath	Whitethorn	May 12
D		Duir	Oak	June 10
T		Tinne	Holly	July 8
C		Coll	Hazel	Aug 5
Q		Quert	Apple	Aug 5

Letter	Ogham	Irish	English	Date
M		Muin	Vine	Sept 2
G		Gort	Ivy	Sep 30
Ng/Gn/P		Ngetal/Peth	Reed	Oct 28
Z/FF(F)		Straif	Blackthorn	April 15
R		Ruis	Elder	Nov 25

Consonants

PAGAN SIGILS

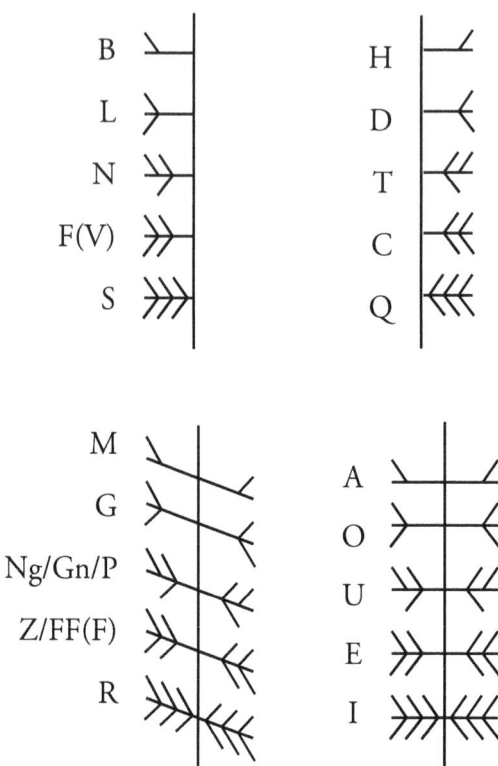

Branching Ogham Fews and Groves

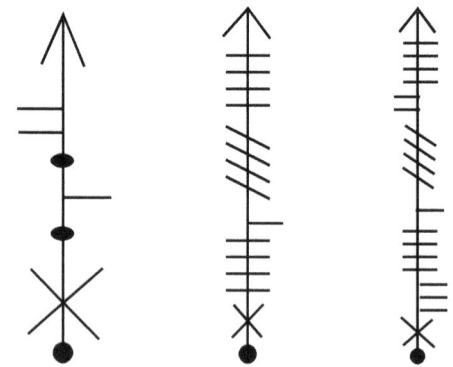

Ogham Staves

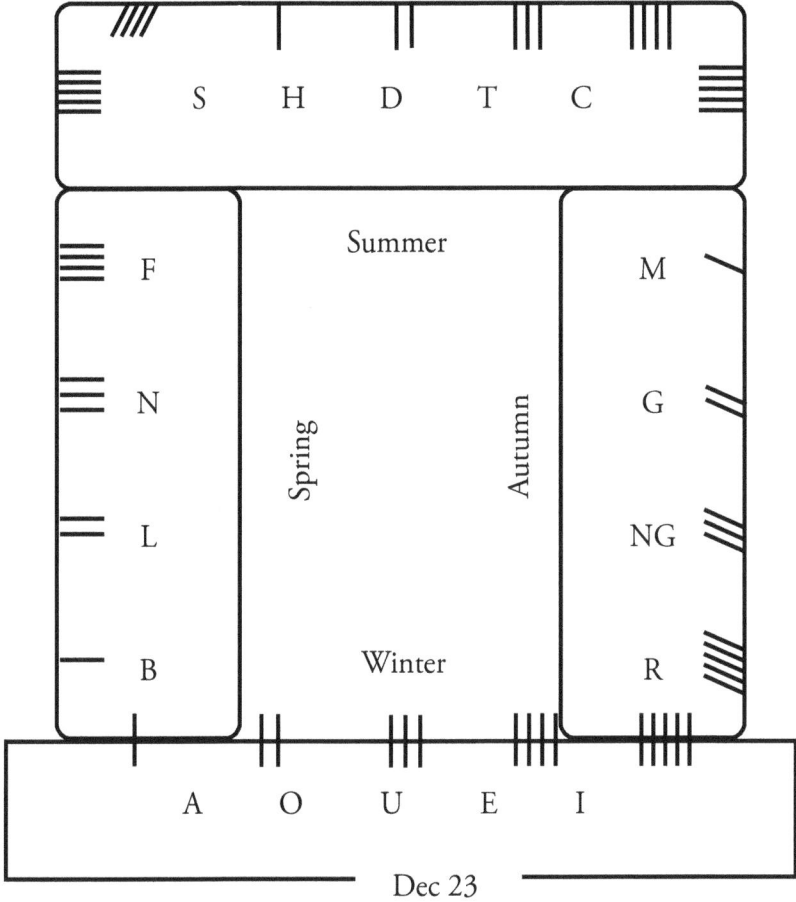

BLNF S(Z)HDTC(Q) MGNgR AOUEI
BLN Lunar Calender

Ogham Henge Arrangement

The tally arrays of Ogham script form individual letters called fews. In the Tree Ogham alphabet there are 20 fews set out into 4 sets of 5 letters called 'groves' that represent the seasons. The fews represent the months, the groves represent the equinoxes and solstices of the lunar and solar calendars. According Robert Graves, British Celts used two versions of the Ogham alphabet. The BLNF was native to Britain, the other was introduced by European Celts.

British Witchcraft

The stereotype of witchcraft is seen as a coven of naked female witches dancing in a circle around a pentagram, worshipping the full moon on the Sabbath and participating in a frenzied sexual orgy with the Devil. A Christian demonization of the Moon Goddess and the fertility rites associated with the Horned God.

Accusations of witchcraft and witch trials were at their height in Britain between 1500 and 1799. Witchcraft was made a capital offence in 1542. It was often seen as a 'healing practise' performed by people called the 'cunning folk', whereas it was later believed to be Satanic in origin, which brought about the persecution of many innocent women, mostly midwives and some men.

At the end of the 18th century, the reasoned thought of the Age of Enlightenment lifted the fear of witchcraft and magic from the human mind, resulting in the Witchcraft Act of England in 1735, that abolished the penalty of execution for witchcraft, replacing it with imprisonment.

Witchcraft continued to be a criminal offence until the repeal of the witchcraft laws in England in 1951, leading to the founding of traditional witchcraft movements and the Wicca religion, consisting of Gardnerian, Alexandrian and other groups.

Traditional British witchcraft is a non Wiccan or pre modern form of the craft, especially if it has been inspired by historical forms of witchcraft and folk magic. Forms of traditional witchcraft include the Feri tradition, Cochranes Craft and the Sabbatic Cult.

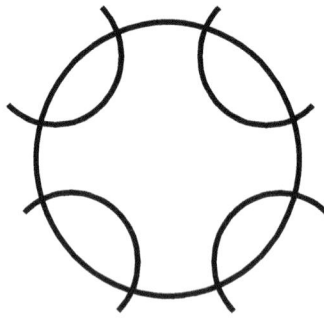

Pagan Wheel of the Year / Well of Wishes / Wiccan Covern

Witch's knot Elven Star

Troll Cross

Witches Knot - Elven Star - Troll Cross

The Witches knot is comprised of four vesca piscis shapes, sometimes with the addition of a central circle. Drawn in one continuous line it is a symbol of protection against witch's. In the Middle Ages it was used by witches to control the weather or as a love charm.

The Elven star is also known as the Faerie star to Wiccans and Pagans. It is symbolic of the number 7, including the Seven Sisters or Pleiades, the 7 planets, 7 precious metals, etc. It was used by Aleistar Crowley in his design for the Astrum Argentum or Silver Star Order. The Troll Cross is an early iron amulet said to give protection against Trolls and mischievous entities.

Hexafoil / Daisy Wheel

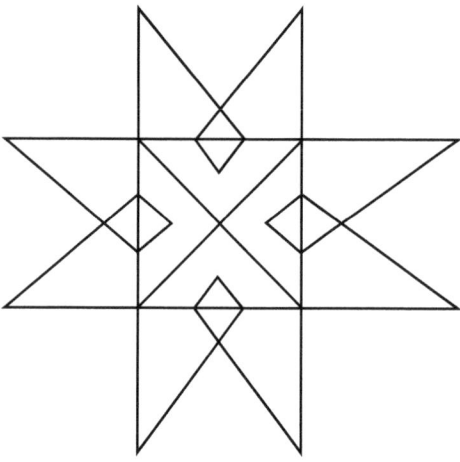

Marian mark

Witches Marks

Apotropatic marks is the name given to 'witches' marks used for protection in buildings and other such structures. They are found scratched or carved into wood, plaster and metal, placed near windows, doors and fireplaces to deter malevolent spirits. Two such common marks are the Hexafoil known as the Daisy Wheel and Marian marks, consisting of overlapping V signs.

PAGAN SIGILS

Witches Circle

The 20th century led to a re-imagining of the witches circle. Nine feet in diameter, it features a pentagram at its center, whose five cardinal points are represented in their associated colour by their symbols or written in runic script. Included are the symbols for the five elements and three degrees of initiation in Gardnerian Wicca.

Witches Sigils

Witches and Wiccans use magic symbols called sigils. A sigil is 'Will and Intent' condensed into one intricate symbol. They can be created using word and letter ciphers or by the graphic binding of letters and/or symbols and signs.

To create a 'word' sigil, first decide upon a key word for the goal sought in a spell, such as CREATE. Find the letters of the word on the Witches Wheel cipher, which consists of three concentric circles that contain the letters of the alphabet. Connect the letters of the word on the wheel with a continuous straight line without taking the pen off the paper. Lines maybe looped around the letters in a witches sigil.

Draw a small circle at the beginning of the line and terminate the end of the line and the sigil is complete. It can be rotated and artistically embellished to increase its magical effect.

Binding is the archaic technique of graphically combining key letters and signs to form a sigil whose power is derived from the magic art of binding. Bind Runes are the most common form of this technique, although alchemical glyphs, signs of the Zodiac, the Planetary symbols and those of the four Elements, can be bound together to form unique glyphs that are sometimes referred to as Elemental sigils.

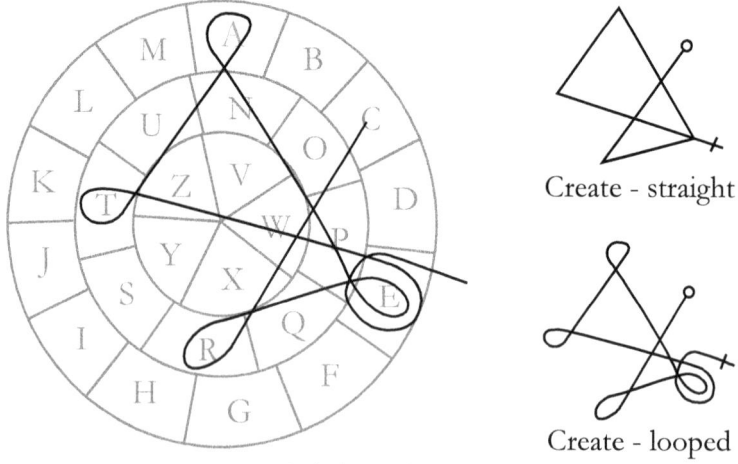

Create - straight

Create - looped

Witches Wheel

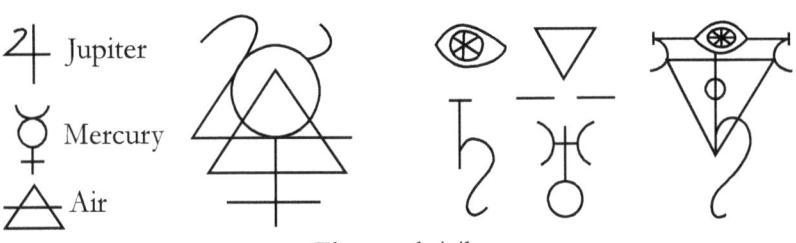

Elemental sigils

Sigils created by modern witches include pictorial devices such as flames, hearts, water droplets, waves, snowflakes, shields, antlers, stars, the sun and the moon. They also contain unique signs for emotions and thoughts. Such sigils can be incorporated into the design of seals, pentacles, amulets and talismans.

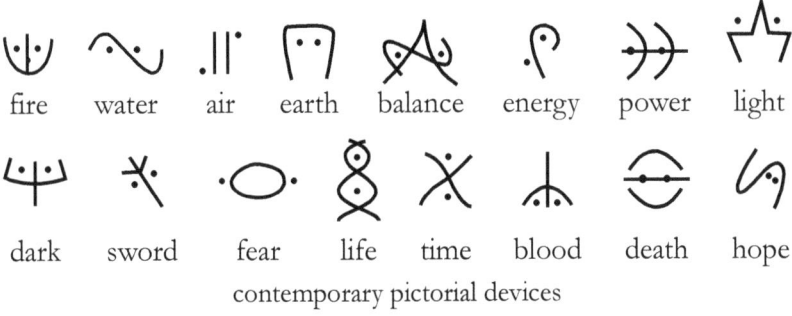

contemporary pictorial devices

Shekinnah
Laura Tempest Zakroff

"May the magik of this Earth flow through my veins from this day until my last"
Brittany Nightshade

Modern Witches sigils

Wicca

Developed in the first half of the 20th century, Wicca is the dominant form of British Neopaganism. Wycca (Wittja) is an old Anglo-Saxon word meaning 'witch'. Although it had various forms in the past, from the 1960s the word 'wicca' was deemed less contentious than the word 'witchcraft'.

It is generally a duotheistic religion, worshiping the Moon Goddess and Horned God. Its Americanization by the popular media has adapted the word to include natural magic or White Witchcraft.

Also called Pagan Witchcraft, Wiccans practise witchcraft and nature worship, especially the tradition founded in England in the mid 20th century. Although Wicca and witchcraft are often used interchangeably, it is important to note that there are also pagan witchcraft traditions that are not Wiccan. Wicca is an initiatory tradition of witchcraft practised as a religion. Religious witchcraft is seen as a pagan mystery religion, worshipping Goddess and God and the Divine in nature.

Wiccans claim its origins lie in pre-Christian, Celtic religion but most witches draw their inspiration from the Book of Shadows, a book of rituals and spells compiled by Gerald Gardner, who is regarded as the father of modern witchcraft.

Born in 1884, he was initiated into the New Forrest Coven of Witches in 1939, from that point on, he devoted himself to promoting his new found religion.

After the war, Gardner wrote a number of books, the best known being Witchcraft Today in 1954. He also formulated the Wiccan calender of eight festivals, bringing together existing festivals from different traditions. He died in 1964.

There are two main forms of Wiccan practised in Britain. Gardnerian Wiccans are those members who can trace their initiatory descent from its founder, Gerald Gardner. Alexandrian Wicca is a tradition founded by Alex Saunders, "The king of Witches" and his wife Maxine. Largely based of Gardnerian Wicca it also contains elements of ceremonial magic and cabala. There are many other forms of Wicca including Faery Wicca.

Gardeners Pentagram

Gardnerian Wicca theories were drawn from various sources including Freemasonry and the Golden Dawn. He was friends with Aleister Crowely who initiated Gardner into the Ordo Templis Orientalis.

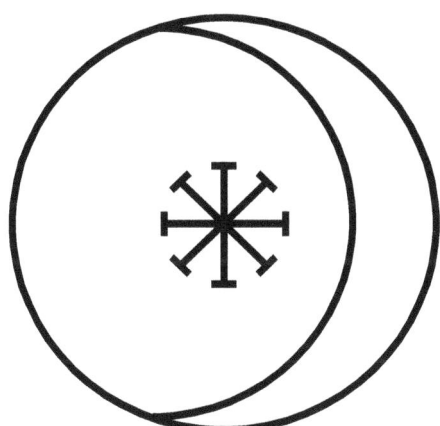

Seax Wicca

A form of Wicca founded in England 1970, based historical Anglo-Saxon paganism. The sigil contains the sun, moon and a star representing the eight wiccan sabbaths.

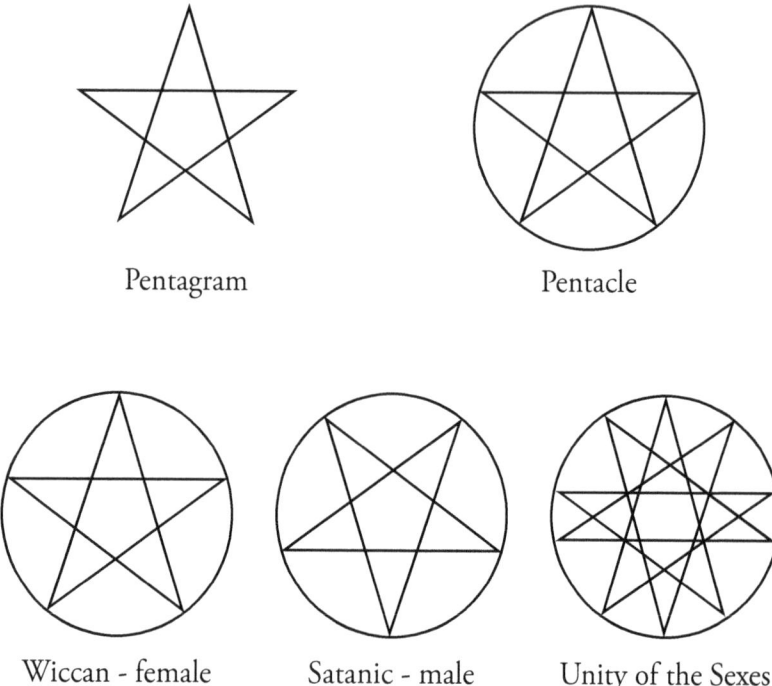

Pentagram

Pentacle

Wiccan - female

Satanic - male

Unity of the Sexes

Pentagram / Pentacle

This ancient five pointed star symbol has always been used to represent the concept of five. It was widely used by Christians up until the 16th century when many Christian symbols became associated with the rise in occult practises.

Wiccans adopted the pentagram, pentacle or five-pointed star as the sign of Venus, both the planet and the Goddess, but the adaptation of the pentagram led to Wicca being seen as Satanic.

The Wiccan pentacle points upwards symbolizing the triumph of spirit over matter. The Satanic pentacle points downwards and represents earthly gratification. Combined as the ten pointed star the pentagrams symbolizes unity of the sexes.

These negative connotations began when the 19th century occultist Eliphas Levi proposed that the inverted pentagram was a sign of evil, without any occult or historical evidence.

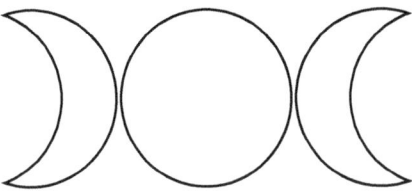

Triple Goddess

Used by many Neopagan and Wiccan groups, this symbol of feminine power represents the Goddess in the three phases of the moon, waxing, full and waning, symbolizing the three life cycles of woman - Maiden - youth, purity, beginnings, Mother - fertility, nurturing, fulfilment, and Crone, wisdom, death and rebirth which combine to represent the Goddess herself. Originally, the Greek Goddess Hera was worshipped as the Maiden, Mother and Widow. In the 20th century Robert Graves used the triple moon to explain the neopagan deity goddess as Mother, Bride and Layer-out.

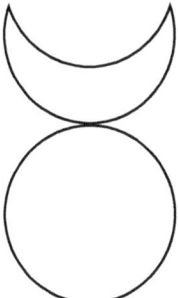

Horned God

A symbol used in Wiccan and other Neopagan groups to represent the masculine energy of the God. An archetypical symbol for vegetation and fertility, it symbolizes July's Horn Moon which is connected to the Goddess.

The symbols has horns but is unrelated to the devil and is similar to the Greek God Pan, half man - half goat of the Shepherds, wilderness and nature. It represents the perfect union of the divine and the animalistic or nature. He also has three phases, Father, Master and Sage.

Goddess Movement

The Goddess movement is a widespread, non-centralised trend in Neopaganism without any centralized tenets of belief. In recent times, many Goddess cults of Europe and the Middle East have being revived in one form or another. Practises vary widely from the name and number of Goddesses worshipped to the specific rituals and rites used to do so.

Most modern pagan traditions honour one or more goddesses. Some follow the Wiccan dualistic system of a single Goddess and a single God that can be recognized as a united whole, others recognise only one or more goddesses. Some such as Dianic Wicca, exclusively worship female deities, while others do not.

In the 19th century, some first wave feminists published their ideas on the female deity. At the same time, anthropologists examined the idea of prehistoric matriarchal culture. It is said that these theologies were suppressed when Christianity outlawed all concepts of there being an ancient religion. These ideas gained greater influence during the second wave of feminism in the 1960s and 70s. Since then, Goddess worship has emerged as a recognizable international cultural movement.

The Goddess Movement includes spiritual beliefs or practises which are chiefly neopagan, emerging throughout North America, Western Europe, Australia and New Zealand at the end of the 20th century. It takes inspiration from the work of archeologists such as Manya Gimbutas whose interpretations of artefacts from Neolithic Europe, reveal human society to be matriarchal or goddess centered, worshipping a female deity of three primary aspects, inspiring neopagan worship of the Triple Goddess.

Goddess religions, especially those that worship a single Great or Mother Goddess emphasize the relationship between femininity and nature. These belief systems honour female energy for its role in fertility and the creation of new life. The Earth is valued as a manifestation of the Goddess and the connection between people, animals and plants. Many people involved in the Goddess Movement regard the Earth as a living goddess.

Dianic Wicca

Dianic Wicca is an eclectic form of British traditional witchcraft, European folk magic, healing practises from various other cultures and feminism. The primary text of Dianic Wicca is the The Holy Book of Women's Mysteries written by it's founder Zsunnanna Bucharest, who self identifies as an 'hereditary witch' claiming to have learnt magic from her mother.

Dianic Wicca began on the winter solstice in 1971 when Budapest led a ceremony in Holywood, California. It developed from the Women's Liberation Movement and covens traditionally align themselves with radical feminism. The majority of Dianic groups reject transgender women due to the tradition's foundation in biological essentialism.

Diana was a Roman Goddess, the daughter of Jupiter and his mistress Latona. She is equated with the Greek Goddess Artemis as a female deity of hunting, the moon, fertility, childbirth and children, the forest and wild animals. She protects mothers and children while embodying purity. Pagans honour Diana on the 13th August, as the original Mother Goddess who epitomizes egalitarian matriarchy.

Divine Feminine Energy

Feminine energy is simply the physical manifestation of all creative energy. Divine feminine energy is the 'true' survival energy. Whereas masculine energy or consciousness works to literally survive and protect the kingdom, the feminine energy or subconscious is the warrior survival energy under pressure. Female energy acknowledges the feminine principal as being the primary aspect of divinity that we experience. It is empowering for a woman to understand the Divine as being female.

In Hinduism, the word Shakti is used to describe the feminine principal energy of the universe. The feminine is always in balance with the masculine known as Shiva. Together they are the cosmic couple and are often shown seated together in spiritual ecstasy, as they symbolizes the union of consciousness and energy, this is Nirvana. Shakti is also the cycle of life, death and rebirth, the endless, unfolding rhythm of creation, sustenance and destruction that exists in all things and also in our life. It is energy and the force in all of its forms.

One of the most important goddesses in the Hindu pantheon, Shakti is a Mahadevi or Great Goddess, the sum of all other goddesses. Every God has a Shakti or energy force and she takes many forms and names. She is honoured as the Mother Goddess, a universal archetype called upon for strength, fertility, power and creativity. As Pavrati she symbolizes fertility, mortal happiness, devotion and asceticism, a powerful female figure who may be called upon to repair or sustain a marriage. As Durga she is a fierce warrior who kills demons and other evil creatures. As Kali she is the Dark Goddess of Destruction, symbolizing the temporary nature of life.

Kali is the Hindu Goddess of Creation and Destruction. Her name means 'black', she has black skin, red eyes, sharp teeth and a protruding tongue, representing the sacred, spoken Sanskrit language. She is sometimes portrayed wearing a necklace of 52 human skulls, each one representing a bija or individual phonetic sound of the Sanskrit language. In Tantra, Kali has her own Yantra and is hailed to be the Divine Essence of the Mother Goddess, the highest reality and the female element known as Shakti or female power. To come face to face with Kali symbolizes a coming to terms with reality.

In classic Jewish thought, Shekhinah refers to a dwelling or settling of divine presence. In some sources, Shekhinah represents the female attributes of the presence of God. Jewish cabala associates Shekhinah with the female and with the most overtly female sephiroth, referred to as the Daughter of God. This is the tenth sephiroth named Malkuth, the source of life for humans on Earth below the sephirotic realm. The harmonious relationship between Shekhinah and the sephiroth that precede her, causes the world itself to be sustained by the flow of divine energy. She is like the moon reflecting the divine light into the world. Moses is the only human known to have risen beyond the Shekhinah into the sephirotic realm, reaching the level of Tiferet or the Bridegroom of the Shekhinah.

The Spiral Goddess is a neopagan symbol representing internal feminine power. The spiral represents creative power within that corresponds to the sacred chakra of menstruation, our desires, our sexuality and our relationships.

Kali Yantra

Spiral Goddess

Primordial / Great / Triple Goddess

Worship of the Primordial Goddess flourished in the Old Stone age when many scholars believe the female body was used to explain the phenomena observed by prehistoric people in nature, reflected in the cycles of the female body such as menstruation, pregnancy, birth and lactation. The tradition of the Primordial Goddess can be seen reflected in many different conceptions of the Divine Feminine including the Great Goddess, the Mother Earth Goddess, the Triple Goddess and the Goddess as the Tree of Life

After 10.000 BCE, humans stopped living a hunter-gatherer nomadic lifestyle and began to live in permanent, organized communities with domesticated animals and the farming of crops. This change brought about a shift in ideology. Although the Primordial Goddess was the original model, as later goddess traditions developed, she was given different roles according to the beliefs and spiritual needs of the people who worshipped her. These roles became aspects of the Divine Feminine before they became separate individuals of a pantheon.

The Great Goddess is the concept of an almighty Goddess or Mother Goddess known in Latin as Magna Dea. She is a postulated fertility goddess supposed to have been worshipped in the Neolithic era across most of Eurasia, at least. She was often a very plump woman associated with snakes, cattle and birds.

In the Greco-Roman pantheon, the Great Goddess Cybele was also associated with Rhea, the mother of the Gods and Gaia, the mother of the Titans. In Hinduism she is the Mahadevi called Shakti, the sum of all Goddesses and the dynamic forces that moves through the Universe.

The Great Goddess is also known as the Triple Goddess, an important deity in Neopaganism and Wicca. This ancient idea first appeared in Egyptian magical papyri but was really popularized by Robert Graves in his book "The White Goddess" published in 1945. It is not uncommon for the Goddess to appear as a triad. The Greek Fates and the Norse Norns fall into this category. Alternatively, one deity can appear in 3 aspects, as with the Greek Goddess Hecate, as Maiden, Mother and Crone or Selene, the

Roman Goddess of the Moon as New, Waxing/Waning and Full. The ancient origins of this threefold idea are reflected in the triple aspect of the Christian male deity as Father, Son and Holy Ghost.

As a reaction to perceptions of predominantly male dominated organized religion, some forms of feminist witchcraft combine the Goddess Movement with political activism. They claim that a male orientated view of divinity only has a history of 5000 years, whereas female divinity goes back at least 7000 years if not 30,000, and has been dismissed as a fertility cult.

They postulate that patriarchy denies the womb, thus denying his own existence. Man cannot exist without the womb. Womb man is the feminine creative source energy that allows man to exist. These divine female figures of ancient history and mythology are becoming role models for pagans and feminists alike.

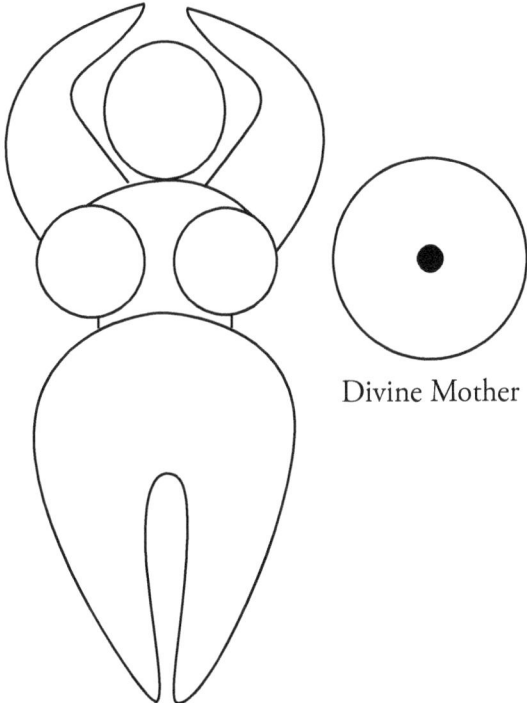

Divine Mother

Primordial Goddess / Great Mother Goddess

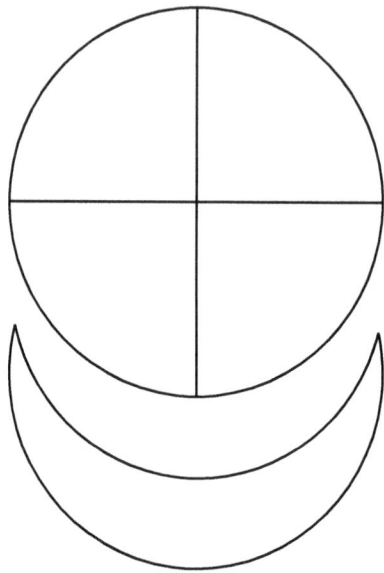

Mother Earth Goddess (Gaia)

The Goddess movement regards Earth as a living Goddess. It is postulated that a Goddess such as "The Mother of All Life" was worshipped as the principal deity for thousands of years in the prehistoric religion of the Earth or Great Mother Goddess, seen as symbolizing the Earth itself.

The figure of the Earth/Mother Goddess date back some 30.000 years to the Paleolithic or Old Stone Age. Ancient religious beliefs recognized that the Goddess was a Divine and sacred female with supernatural powers. A primordial being worshipped as the source of all life.

Gaia or Gaea was the Greek Goddess of the Earth, She was one of the primordial elemental deities born at the dawn of creation. Gaia was the Great Mother of Creation, the Heavenly Gods were descended from her by her union with the Sky (Oranos, Uranus), the sea gods from her union with the Sea (Pontos), the Gigantees or Giants from her union with Tartaros (the Pit, underworld), and mortal creatures are born directly from her earthly flesh. She is symbolically pictured with the seasons, fruits and grains.

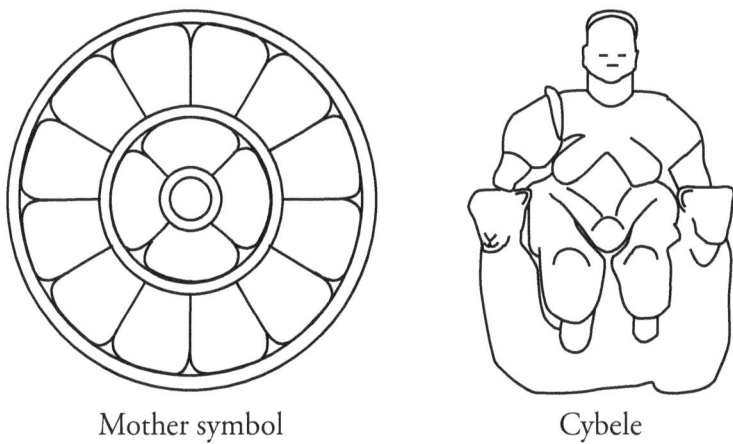

Mother symbol   Cybele

Mother Goddess (Cybele)

The most widely worshiped Great Goddess of the Classical world was Cybele. Originally an Anatolian Mother Goddess, her forerunner may have been found in the earliest Neolithic culture at Catalhuyuk, where statues of a plump woman have been found in excavation. Cybele is the only known Phygrian Goddess and was probably a national deity. Greeks living in Asia Minor adopted her and developed her cult, taking it to mainland Greece and to their western colony in Italy.

In Greece she became assumed into the aspect of the Earth Goddess Gaia, the Minoan equivalent Rhea and the Harvest Mother Demeter. In Athens, she was portrayed as an essentially foreign, exotic mystery goddess who arrives on a chariot drawn by lions. Unusually for the Greeks, she had a eunuch priesthood and included rites to a divine Phygrian castrate, shepherd consort called Attis, who was probably a Greek invention. In Greece, Cybele was associated with mountains, towns and cities, fertile nature and animals, especially lions.

In Rome, Cybele became known as Magna Mater or the Great Mother and was conscripted as a key religious ally in the war against Carthage. The Romans revered her as a Trojan goddess and ancestral to Rome by way of the Trojan prince Aeneas.

Asherah

Asherah is an ancient Semitic Mother Goddess, who appears in a number of ancient sources, in which she is identified as the consort of the highest ranking Mesopotamian God called Anu. In Sumerian sources her name is Antu, wife of Anu. In Ugarit, (modern Lebanon) she was the wife of El, also the highest ranking god of the pantheon. Asherah was worshipped within the household and her offerings were performed by family matriarchs.

In the 1960s, the notion of a Jewish historical Mother Goddess was popularized in the USA by Raphael Pata in his publication 'The Hebrew Goddess' which focused on the cult of Hebrew Goddesses such as the cult of Asherah, who is sometimes symbolized by the Tree of Life.

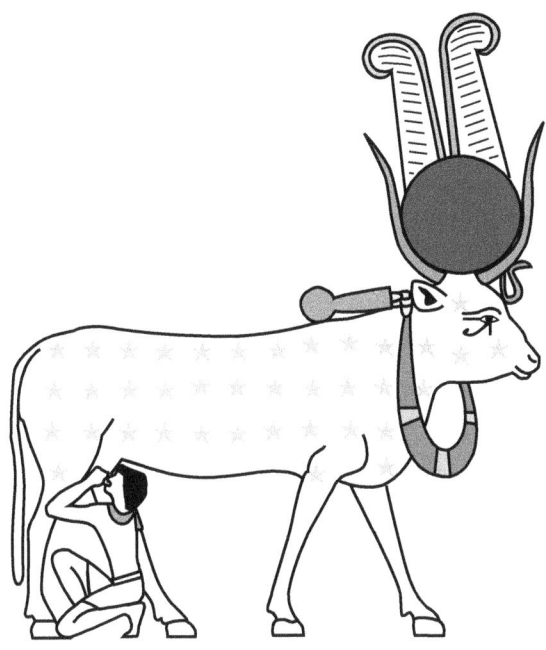

Hathor

One of the 42 state deities of ancient Egypt and one of the most powerful, Hathor was the Goddess of love, beauty, music, dancing, fertility and pleasure. She was a protector of women although men also worshipped her. She was a daughter of Ra and was sometimes called the Eye of Ra, along with the other deities whose role was the Sun God's defender. Her name, Hathor translates as House of Horus. She was the wife of Horus and associated with the mother of the Pharaoh in her role as nurse to Horus, and also with the wife of Pharaoh in her role as the consort of Horus.

According to Egyptian myth, Hathor personified the sky, and was portrayed as a cow who possessed the four legs that maintained the firment of Heaven. The cow was also symbolic of her maternal and sublime character, although she was usually represented as a woman wearing a crown of cows horns and a solar disc. In her role as the Goddess of Beauty, she was the patron of cosmetics and wearing cosmetics was seen as a form of Hathor worship. Offerings of mirror's and cosmetic palette's to her were common.

Isis / Eset

Isis is the Greek name for the Egyptian Goddess Eset, the supreme Mother Goddess, sister/consort of her husband/brother Osiris and the mother of their son Horus. As the mother of Horus, she was considered to be the divine mother of the Pharaoh, who was likened to Horus. Her worship was not restricted to Egypt, her influence spread throughout the Greco-Roman world as far as the Rhine, where she was called the Star of the Sea, a title also given to Mary the Mother of Christ.

Isis was first mentioned in the Old Kingdom texts circa 2500 BCE, as one of the main characters in the Osiris myth, in which she is denoted by a Throne symbol headdress. During the New Kingdom circa 1250 BCE, she took on traits that originally belonged to the pre-eminent Egyptian Mother Goddess Hathor, symbolized by her cow horns and lunar headdress.

By the first millennium BCE, Isis and Osiris were the most widely worshipped Egyptian deities. This was when her reputed magic power was greater than that of all other Gods, having the power over fate itself. She was invoked in healing spells, funerary rites and magical texts.

Worshipped by both Egyptians and Greeks during the Hellenistic period, by the first half of the 1st century CE, the cult of Isis had become a part of Roman religion, where some of her devotees claimed she encapsulated all the divine powers in the world. The worship of Isis was ended by the rise of Christianity in the 4th to 6th centuries CE but her worship may have influenced Christian beliefs such as the veneration of Mary. Isis continued to appear in western culture, particularly in esotericism and modern paganism

The concept of a single goddess incorporating all feminine divine power became widespread among groups and individuals like the Hermetic Order of the Golden Dawn in the late 19th century and Dion Fortune in 1930s, adopted the all-encopassing goddess into their belief systems and called her Isis. This conception of Isis influenced the concept of the Great Goddess found in many forms of contemporary witchcraft.

Hathor   Isis / Eset

Goddess of Love and War

Modern pagan feminists see the Goddess of Love and War as a powerful female protagonist, who engaged both mentally and physically with the male members of her family, to achieve her independence, equal status and rightful possession. As the Goddess of Love she was related to romantic and sexual love through her lover and familiar love or the love between communities.

In love magic, her powers could alter romantic fortunes. In ancient love charms her influence was invoked to win or indeed capture the heart or any other body part of a desired lover. As a War Goddess, she was seen to have a potent capacity for revenge. On the battlefield, the Goddesses ability to fix fates ensured victory. She is the archetypical rose covered in thorns.

The original Goddess of Love and War was the Mesopotamian deity known as Inanna. She also appears under the names of Ishtar and Astarte and is associated with Aphrodite/Venus. Her sacred city was called Erech which translates as Town of the Sacred Courtesans, or Sacred Prostitutes.

In Erech, the priestesses of the temple of Ishtar carried out sacred prostitution as a profound fertility rite. Ishtar as a Goddess was highly sexually charged and was vilified by the Christian faith as the Whore of Babylon and the Mother of Harlots, despite the fact she was worshipped in Jerusalem as the Queen of Heaven. The word Harlot means Sacred Prostitute or Holy Woman.

Inanna was one of the most popular deities in the Sumerian pantheon. Yet in the modern day, she has slipped into almost total anonymity. Her legacy is most clearly seen through her influence on later cultural archetypes, most significantly controlling the development of the Greco-Roman Goddess of Love known as Aphrodite/Venus.

One of her Semitic cultural archetypes was Ba'alat Gubal, the Goddess of the city of Gubal, also known as Byblos in Phoenicia, that now equates to modern Lebanon. She was generally identified with the pan-Semitic Goddess Astate or Ashtart and equated with the Greco-Roman Aphrodite/Venus. Alternatively, the Phoenician author Sanchuniathon presents Ba'alat Gubal as a sister of Astarte

Star of Inanna / Ishtar

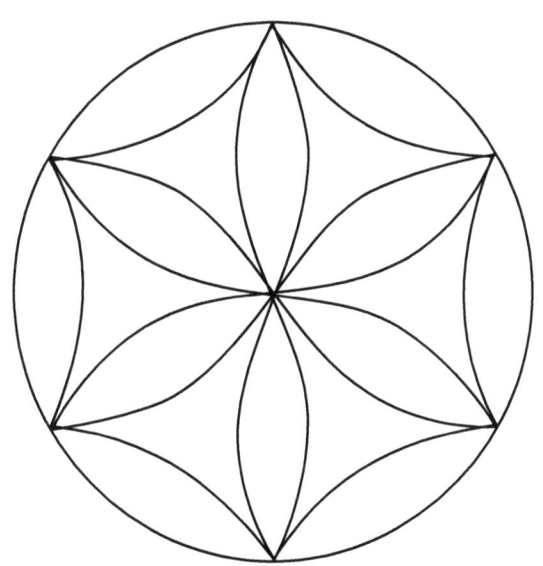

Aphrodite / Venus

and Asherah, calling Ba'alat Gubal by the name Dione, the sister of the Great God El, whom she had daughters with. She is also equated with the Egyptian Mother Goddess Hathor/Isis.

Another Semitic cultural archetype thought to be an aspect of the Phoenician Goddess Astarte, is the Punic Goddess Tannit and alongside her consort Baal Hamon, they were the city deities of Carthage (Tunisia). In Carthage, it is thought her temple was used to offer up the bodies of children who had died naturally during childbirth or at a very early age. This led to accusations of child sacrifice and witchcraft by the Romans.

The Carthaginians spread the cult of Tannit across North Africa to Sicily, Malta and Spain, where she was assimilated into local nature deities. After the Roman conquest, she was integrated with the Roman Goddess Juno, where she remained a deity of the moon, sexuality, fertility and war. In Ibiza, there are efforts to resurrect her worship.

The Church of the Guanche is a neopagan religious organization founded in the Canary Islands in 2001, by a group of Canarian devotees of the Goddess Chaxiraxi. Chaxiraxi is a Goddess known as the Sun Mother in the religion of the aboriginal Graunche inhabitants and the principle deity of their pantheon.

Matriarchal Heathenism is the foundation of the native Cervanche people of the Canary Islands They are believed to have been precivilization Berbers from North Africa. It is conjectured that Chaxiraxi may have been adapted from the Punic-Berber Goddess Tannit and given a new name and attributes.

PAGAN SIGILS

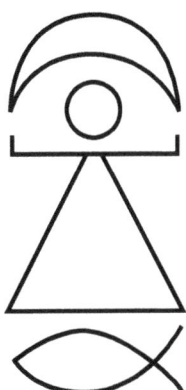

Ba'alat Gubal

Tannit

Chaxiraxi

Witch Goddesses

Scholars believe that the concept of the witch dates back as long as humans have worshipped deities. In ancient Egypt the word for magic was Hekka. In Greek mythology the first witch was Hekate, Goddess of Magic and Astrology. In most traditions witches were holy women or wise women, interpreters of dreams and skilled healers and midwives, proficient in herbal medicine.

By the 1400s, the rise of male centered Christianity and the growth of early capitalism, led to the demonization of powerful women in the Middle Ages.

The publication of Malleus Maleficourus or Hammer for Witches, a medieval treatise on how to 'hunt' witches, by German churchman Heinrich Krammer, inflamed the mass hysteria that accompanied European witchunts between 1500 and 1600 CE.

Across the continent, local governments murdered up to 80,000 innocent women and men thought to be witches. The infamous Salem witch trails of the USA took place in the 1690s with local women accused of devil worship.

In the modern world, the political disenfranchisement of women is given as one reason why women are turning to witchcraft. Along with other marginalized groups such as the LGBT community. The witch pushes back against social norms such as marriage and child bearing, instead it reinforces a bond between women that can range from friendship to sexual love.

Medieval legends said that all witches are descended from the biblical Lilith. Her refusal to lie beneath Adam set the archetypical example for later feminists.

Hekate is the Greek Goddess of the Moon and the Underworld, who is often among those referred to as the Triple Goddess. She is also the Queen of Witches and has two opposing aspects, one who brings about prosperity, protection at sea and a bountiful harvest. The other is a terrifying, demonic aspect as the Goddess of Death, associated with ghosts and nightmares. She haunts crossroads, graveyards and tombs and often appears with her pack of Hellhounds. As the Mistress of Sorcery, she is summoned by incantations and presides over spells, charms and all enchantments.

Circe was the daughter of the Greek Sun God Helios and the sea nymph Perse, although some writers say she was born to Hekate. Circe was an enchantress who possessed a magic wand and concocted magic potions. She is most famous for transforming people into animals. In one version of her myth, she brings her consort Odysseus back from the dead, using her magic powers and herbs.

Cerridwen is the Celtic Goddess of Magic, her name is derived from the Celtic word 'cerri' meaning 'cauldron', symbolizing the transformative powers of magic, wisdom, rebirth and creative inspiration. Another Celtic Goddess associated with magic, fertility and feminine power is Epona, the Horse Goddess who was also associated with the night and dreams.

In Norse mythology, the fertility Goddess Freyja was also the Goddess of Magic, who knew the art of prophecy. Her knowledge was at least equal to that of Odin but she never revealed her secrets or tried to change events she knew were inevitable. Freyja was also a Goddess of War, half the warriors slain in battle go to her sacred meadow of Folkvong.

The demonizing, patriarchal readings of myths associated with the first human woman are exposed by pagan feminists thus. Pandora like Eve, was of the first race of womb men. Pandora was created as a punishment, as was Eve. Their sin marked the end of paradise. Both were curious, both broke their word, releasing all the sorrows of the human condition. In the Pandora myth, only Hope remained.

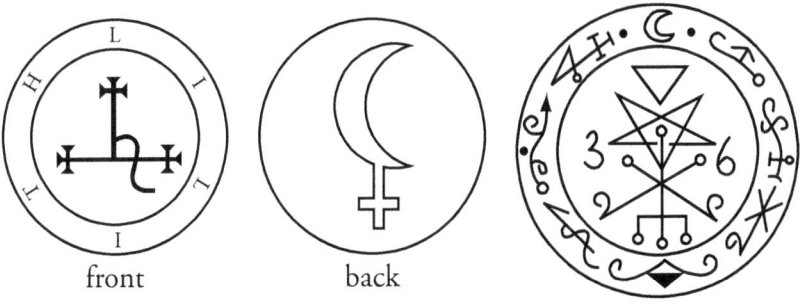

front   back

Medieval Seals of Lilith

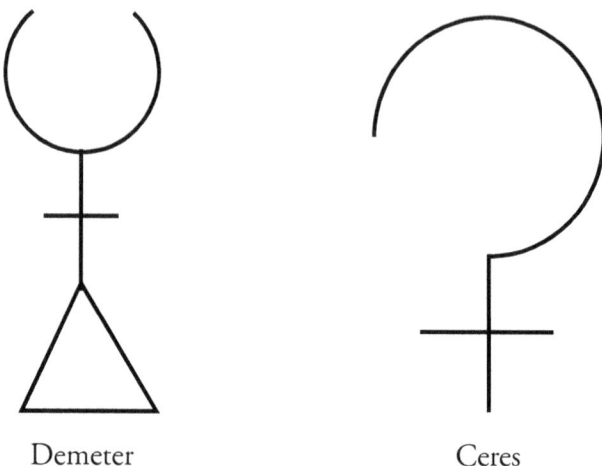

Demeter   Ceres

Harvest Goddess - Demeter / Ceres

Agricultural deities are linked to the Earth Goddess. Harvest is the end of summer, one of the four seasons that belong to the Earth Goddess. Such deities are associated with fertility, reward/harvest, fruits and grains, especially corn. Isis annually flooded the Nile and taught women how to grind and store corn.

Demeter is the Greek Goddess of the Harvest and is considered to be the same figure as the Anatolian Mother Earth Goddess Cybele. Ceres was one of many Roman agricultural deities and is seen as their counterpart to the Greek Demeter, whose mythology was reinterpreted for Ceres by the Romans. As the Goddess of agriculture, grain crops and motherly relationships, she was worshiped in her seven day April festival Cerelia, at harvest time, during marriages and funeral rites and at other times of the year.

Over the millennia, many names of Greco-Roman Goddesses have been used to identify various astronomical phenomena such as planets, meteors, asteroids, lunar nodes etc. These symbols are available on the internet and have been a source of graphic reference for neopagans.

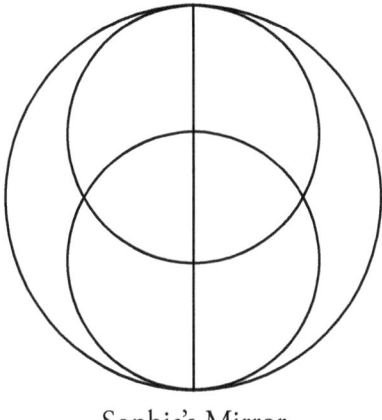

Sophia's Mirror

Wisdom Goddess - Athene / Minerva - Sophia

Wisdom is a gift often attributed to the Warrior Goddess as well as those deities whose realm is the intellect. Athene was the Greek Goddess of Wisdom, her Roman equivalent was Minerva. Athene was portrayed with a spear, shield and owl, protecting the ancient city of Athens. Athene ruled by reason rather than emotion or compassion, brushing aside romance, marriage and motherhood she was given the title of Virgin Goddess. Feminists relate to her as a role model for the modern independent woman.

Sophia meaning 'wisdom', is a Greek Goddess who is a central idea in Hellenistic philosophy, Platonism, Gnosticism and Christian theology. Originally, Sophia meant 'cleverness, skill', the later meaning of wisdom or intelligence was significantly shaped by the term 'philosophy' meaning 'love of wisdom' as used by Plato.

In the Christian world, Sophia is the personification of divine wisdom as Holy Wisdom or Hagia Sophia. In Hebrew she is referred to as Achamoth or Chockmah. In Gnostocism, Sophia is not only anologous to the human soul but simultaneously one of the feminine aspects of God. Gnostics held that she is a Bride of Christ and the Holy Spirit of the Trinity. She is the lowest aeon or anthropic expression of the emanation of the Light of God. Sophia is considered to have fallen from grace in some way, in so doing creating or helping to create the material world.

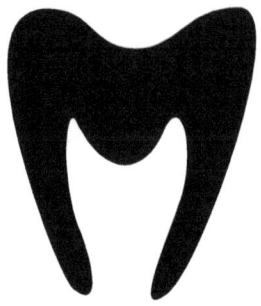

Yoni

The Goddess movement has appropriated many symbols for the feminine and motherhood. Yoni is a Hindu Sanskrit word meaning 'womb' or 'source', the female organs of generation. It is an abstraction or aniconic representation of the Goddess Shakti. It is usually shown with 'linga' its masculine counterpart. The Yoni is conceptualized as nature's gateway to all births, particularly in the esoteric Kaula, Tantra, Shaktism and Shavism.

Asase Ye Duru

Meaning 'the world has weight', this Adrinka sign symbolizes providence and Mother Earth. These Ghanaian symbols encapsulate and evocate messages conveying traditional wisdom, philosophy, theories, ideas or aspects of life or the environment. These once obscure symbols now appear in Holywood movies.

Tapuat

This Hopi symbol depicts a maze or labyrinth representing the relationship between mother and child. Beginning at the center and radiating outwards as the child's world expands. Life may sometimes feel like a maze and the Hopi are aware of this. At a higher level, the Tapuat represents Mother Earth or the Cosmic Mother (the Universe). It is a symbol of birth and rebirth.

Celtic Motherhood Knots

These contemporary Celtic knot designs symbolize Motherhood. The first knot consists of two interwoven hearts, the inner heart is the child and the outer heart, the mother.

The second knot is formed by five vesci piscis. Four of which form the Mother. Two of these intertwine to form a central vesci pescis representing the child. Both knots are bound together so there is no start or finish in them, representing eternity.

Cowrie Shell

More than any other shell, the Cowrie has a marked resemblance to the female genitalia or Yoni. Because of the ancient idea of the Doctrine of Signatures, the shell is therefore endowed with magical powers of fertility, good luck and wealth. Originating from the Malaysian area, cowrie shells were used as currency for some time. Their use in decorative masks, headdresses and other items was widespread, where it had the new addition of being a status symbol because of its use as small change. The Cowrie also represents the eye and protects against evil.

Scallop Shell

The scallop is home to the mussel, a marine creature that, like all other animals that inhabit a very watery environment, is associated with the moon and the eternal feminine. The personification of this idea is found in Botticelli's painting 'the birth of Venus' as the Goddess rises from the ocean standing on top of a scallop shell. The shell is shaped like the female sex organ. Pearls also grow within these shells. Mary the Mother carried a precious pearl within her womb, hence the symbol on the cap of the pilgrim.

Earth Religions

Earth-centered or Nature Worship is a religious system based on the veneration of natural phenomena. It covers only religions that worship the earth, nature or a fertility deity such as the various forms of Goddess worship or Matriarchal religions. Earth religions are also formulated to allow one to utilize the knowledge of preserving the Earth.

There are many thoughts on the origins of Earth religions. One of which claims that pre-Indo-European societies lived in small scale, family based communities that practised matrilineal succession and goddess centered religions in which woman is the Creator. The Divine Mother who can give and take away.

Another origin states that, because human existence depends on nature, men began to form their religion and beliefs on and around nature itself to form nature worship.

Although Earth religion has been around for thousands of years, it first came to the fore in the modern world during the second half of the 20th century, in the late 1960s and early 70s, as part of the New Age movement that grew out of Counter Culture. Because of the vast diversity of religions that fall into this category, there is no consensus of beliefs, however, the ethical beliefs of most of them overlap. The most well known ethical codes are the Wiccan Rede and the Threefold Law.

Mother Nature
(Tortuga/Turtle)

Mother Nature
(Gaia)

Luciferianism and Satanism

According to the Christian church, Devil worship has always existed and is a continual threat to the Kingdom of God's Heaven. Prior to the 20th century, Luciferianism was a form of medieval neo-gnosticism and Satanism didn't exist.

Both cults have their roots in the antithesis or anti-hero of the Christian God. Luciferianisn began in the 13th or 14th century, attributed to a woman called Lucardis who wanted to restore Lucifer to his righteous place in Heaven.

For medieval neo-gnostic sects like the Bogomills, Cathars and Luciferians, Lucifer is the true God and the Old Testament God is the Demiurge, the Devil, the one responsible for imprisoning mankind in the material world.

Satan on the other hand is a modern construct based on religious, historical, artistic and philosophical interpretations of the central figure of evil in Christianity.

This tradition began in the 14th century and remained unacknowledged until a resurgence in the 19th century. After which modern personalities such as Aleistar Crowley, Anton Le Vey and Sloane developed its philosophies and initiated its Bible, Church and Temples. Most infamously, Le Vey compiled the Satanic Bible and set up the Church of Satan in the USA in the late 1960s.

Over the centuries, Lucifer and Satan have been classified by demonologist as Princes of Hell along with other senior demons including Leviathan, Beelzebub and Belial. Others nominations include Asmodus, Belpheger, Mamon, Paimon and Astaroth, formally the Goddess Astarte.

Baphomet is a deity of the classical Levant - Palestine, Lebanon, Israel, Jordan. Knowledge of him was brought back to Europe by the Templars, who were then persecuted by the Christian church for their supposed worship of him. Behemoth is mentioned in Milton's Paradise Lost and in the Dictionaire Infernal.

At the beginning of the 21st century, a myriad of new Satanic sects exist in Europe, America and Australasia with widely different philosophies on the nature of their chosen deity.

Devil Sigils

Both Lucifer and Satan are represented using the same alchemical glyphs for Sulphur, associated with the Fire and Brimstone of Hell. Only Lucifer is associated with the light of Phosphorous.

Sigillum Diabolus (full sigil of Lucifer)

Sigil of Lucifer

The Sigillum Diabolus was first documented in the Grimoirium Verum, the Grimoire of Truth, published in 1517. He is part of the evil three along with Beelzebub and Astaroth.

The sigils purpose was to be an instrument of visual innovation, a gateway, to invoke the presence of Lucifer. In modern times it has been adopted by Satanic and Luciferian cults as an emblem.

The sigil of Lucifer's graphic appearance is that of a chalice representing creation, the fertile darkness awaiting and ready for untold possibilities, as He is the bearer of light and wisdom into the darkness (that has been invoked by this sigil).

The X over the chalice indicates the power and realm of the physical plane, as it is passion and sensuality that drives all entities. The inverted triangle represents Water, often referred to as the 'original elixir of life' without which physical life could not exist. The V at the bottom of the sigil represents the duality of all things, and as the power of convergence of the two into one manifesting balance, creation and existence.

Sigil of Beelzebub

Beelzebub, originally thought to have meant Lord of the High Place (Heaven), is the name of a deity worshipped in the Philistine city of Ekron. The name we have now is probably a Hebrew variation designed to denigrate the deity as Lord of the Flies. In Christian texts, the name was that of a demon or devil. Jesus was accused of being an agent of Beelzebub, Prince of Demons. In Medieval times, he was seen as one of the Chief Demons of Hell and was also associated with witchcraft.

Sigil of Astaroth

Along with Lucifer and Beelzebub, Astaroth is a Great Duke of Hell in the first hierarchy, part of the evil three. In cabala, he is an archdemon associated with the adverse forces or Qliphoth. In the Grimoirium Verum, he is the infernal principality which rules the Americas. His name is thought to be derived from the Hebrew version for the Phoenician Goddess Astarte (Ishtar, Inanna). The Christian Church re-classified her as the male demon Astaroth, one of the 72 Goetic demons of Solomonic ceremonial magic.

Leviathan Cross

Also known as the Crux Satana or Satan's Cross, this elaborate symbol features two bars on the upright cross, symbolizing double protection and a balance between male and female. At the bottom of the cross is the Infinity sign which also becomes the double Ouroboros. The cross also carries phallic connotations.

In alchemy, the Leviathan Cross is the symbol for Sulphur, one of the three essential elements of Nature, along with Salt and Mercury. The cross was originally used by both the Knights Templar and the Cathars, but there is no record of this particular cross having any connections to Satanism, prior to its adoption by Anton Le Vey as a symbol for his Church of Satan.

Sigil of Baphomet

The Sigil of Baphomet was a 19th century French design called the Goat of Mendes, comprised of the head of a goat transfixed upon a reversed pentagram flanked by Hebrew letters of the word 'Leviathan'. Another version shows the names Samuel and Lilith in the center circle. It was adopted as the official emblem of the Church of Satan by Anton Le Vey in the 1960s.

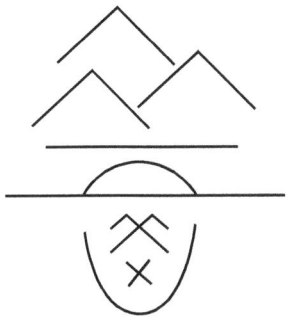

Original Sigil of Behemoth

Behemoth is a large, powerful entity, a Great Beast from the Book of Job, the form of the primeval chaos monster created by God at the beginning of Creation. He is paired with the other monster called Leviathan.

Red King

The Red King is a symbol for Sulphur. This symbol of a fire triangle with three radiating triangles below represents the perfect Red King - the Sulphur of the Philosophies - used to summon the angel Gabriel. Because of its association with sulphur it has been adopted by Satanists and used by some as a Sigil of Behemoth.

Mark of the Beast

Created by Aleister Crowley, the self-styled Great Beast himself, the Mark of the Beast effectively became his own personal sign. It combines signs for the sun and crescent moon with three overlapping circles on top of a septagram or 7 pointed star and the number 666 on its downward point. It is believed to symbolize Crowley's fascination with sex magick.

Sigil of the Satanic Temple

The Satanic Temple was founded in 2013 and recognized as a Church by the US IRS in 2019. They do not believe in a supernatural Satan, it uses the literary Satan as a metaphor to promote pragmatic scepticism and freedom issues, using Satan as a symbol representing the eternal rebel against arbitrary authority and social norms. Their sigil is a reworking of the Sigil of Baphomet, featuring a goats skull in place of the Goat of Mendes head and the letters T S T around it.

original 60s design   70s redesign

Process Church of the Final Judgement

The Process Church was originally a religious movement founded in Mayfair, London 1966, by two former scientologists. It spread to the USA, where it developed Satanic and Nazi associations. It became the most infamous Satanic cult of the 1960s, associated with the Charles Manson Family murders which led to their demise. Their logo consisted of four rotating letter P's. It was redesigned in the early 70s.

Septenary Sigil

The Septenary sigil is the logo of the Order of Nine Angels, a neo-Satanic and left handed cult originating in England with chapters across the world. Beginning in the 1960s, it rose to prominence during the 1980s for having associations with extreme rightwing philosophies, although it describes its approach as traditional Satanism. The Septenary Star symbolizes the Orders Cosmic Tree and the seven planets, as a basis for explaining their sevenfold mystical system.

Neoshamanism

In common with other Neopagan and New Age movements, Neoshamanism is a eclectic synthesis based on a reinterpretation of traditional shamanic practises.

In the second half of the 20th century, Westerners involved in Counter Culture movements were inspired to create modern magico-religious practises influenced by their idea of indigenous religions from across the world, creating what has been termed Neoshamanism or the Neoshamanic movement.

This has affected the development of many neopagan practices, as well as accusations of cultural appropriation, exploitation and misrepresentation when outside observers have tried to represent cultures to which they do not belong.

Shamanic practises have been a part of human consciousness for millennia. A shaman acts as a medium between the visible world and the spirit world. They practise rituals to ensure good health, bountiful harvests, successful hunts and good weather.

Neoshamanism draws heavily from traditional shamanism. In Europe, it is from the nomadic traditions of Siberia and the Sami (Laplanders) of the Arctic circle. In the America's, it is those of Amazonian, Mesoamerican and Native American traditions.

The Shamanic Renaissance emerged in the 1970s, born out of 1960s Counter Culture with its dismissal of mainstream society and politics, and adoption of New Age spirituality and values. There are overlaps, especially in the use of symbols between Neoshamanism, Neopaganism and the New Age, all of which have been subsumed under the heading of nature religion, the belief in an interconnected and sacred Universe.

Neoshamanism or Western shamanism seeks to reclaim what they see as a lost heritage. The Neoshamanic movement primarily originated in the UK, USA and NW Europe but is not limited to those parts of the globe. A major Neoshamanic movement in Latin America is El Camino Rojo or The Red Path, a mixture of pan-Indian and New Age practises.

Neoshamanism comprises an eclectic range of beliefs and practises that involve attempts to attain altered states and communication with the spirit world through drumming, rattling, dancing, chanting, music and psychoactive substances.

Neoshamanists also conduct 'soul retrievals' based on their interpretation of Native American 'sweat lodge' ceremonies and participate in drum circles. This experience of synthesis is comparable with other traditional shamanic practise and those of the contemporary theology of Core Shamanism.

Core Shamanism is a conservative, purist approach to shamanism, originated by Michael Harner in the 1970s from the Counter Culture movement of the 1960s. It is the Neoshamanic system most widely used in the West and has had a profound impact on Neoshamanism. His invention is a decontextualized and appropriated structure similar to the Amazonian Ayahuaca ceremonies of drinking psychoactive teas.

Since the West lost its shamanic knowledge centuries ago due to religious oppression, the foundation of Core Shamanism is particularly intended for Westerners to reacquire access to their rightful spiritual heritage, through quality guided workshops and ceremonial work.

It differs from Neoshamanism which uses metaphorical images and idealized concepts of shamanism, which are joined with beliefs and diverse ritual that have little to do with traditional shamanism. There are some areas overlapping between the two forms but they are different.

Traditional shamans are chosen by the community or inherit the title or both. In Neoshamanism anybody can be a shaman. In a traditional context, shaman are culturally recognized social and ceremonial roles, that seek the assistance of spirits to maintain cosmic order and balance. In Neoshamanism, the focus is usually on personal exploration and development.

Some Neoshamans profess to enact shamanic ceremonies in order to heal others and the environment, but the majority of them practise in isolation and the people they work on are paying customers. This has caused some Native American's to label Neoshamanism as Plastic Medicine.

Neoshamanic Symbols

Symbols are the way our ancestors took all the information as energy and put it into symbols, designed to a specific effect using efficient means. Sometimes spirits are influenced by the use of symbols that resonate with their energy and it can lead to working with them. Other times, symbols can protect one from the energies of spirits one doesn't want to engage with.

Many symbols used by ancestral shamans have been passed down through generations of bloodline, gaining power through each generation continuing the tradition.

Neoshamanism has an eclecticism that takes the symbolism of indigenous and tribal cultures and employs them to create symbology that appeals to the western mind, in the same manner as does the New Age.

At the other extreme, individual Neoshaman claim to have been given power symbols by the spirits to use in their shamannic practises which they feature on their web sites.

The Quinterium is a Neoshamanic symbol given to Shaman Durek.com. A spirit asked him to create the symbol and then bury it for 17 years before bringing it into the world. According to Shaman Durek, the Quinterium holds all the energy of all the elements. It connects all the different spiritual realms in all directions including above and below. It holds the foundation of ancient wisdom, of ancient healing and connection to the elements and the essence of life itself.

The Shamanic Helper is a symbol given by a spirit called 'Rains Again' as a symbol of shamanic power. Another shamanic power symbol is the Shamanic Flame symbol.

Life and Earth - Core Shamanism

PAGAN SIGILS

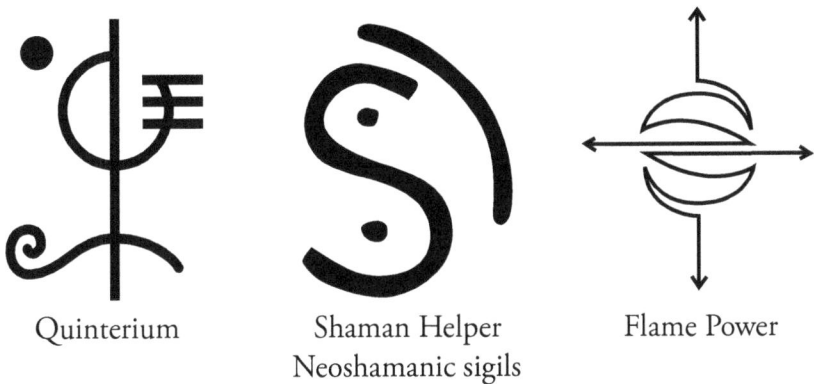

Quinterium   Shaman Helper   Flame Power
                Neoshamanic sigils

Neoshamanic drum featuring the combined
Hopi fertility symbols for Kokopelli and the Tauput

Traditional Shamanism

Traditional shamanism is a religious practise that involves a practitioner who is believed to interact with a spirit world through altered states of consciousness such as a trance. The aim of this is usually to divert these spirit or spiritual energies into the physical world for healing or other purposes.

Shamanistic practises may date back as far as the Paleolithic era circa 30,000 BCE and certainly to the Neolithic era, predating all other religions. Historically, shamanism is associated with indigenous and tribal societies and involves the belief that Shaman with a connection to the other world have the power to heal the sick, communicate with spirits, and escorts the souls of the dead to the afterlife.

Traditional shamanism is declining around the world as entire belief systems have been eroded and endangered by religious and political imperialism and its practitioners and communities grow old and lose their memories. Only those peoples who could preserve their isolation until the 20th century resisted.

Isolated groups such as the nomadic Tuva of Russia have managed to preserve the art of shamanism until today, due to their isolation, allowing them to be free from the influence of other major religions and political influences.

Following this decline, there are revitalization and tradition preserving efforts as a response. Many communities are undergoing resurgence through self-determination and the reclamation of dynamic traditions. However, they are overwhelmed by fraudulent shaman or plastic medicine men.

Besides tradition preserving efforts, there are also neoshamanic movements that differ from many traditional shamanic practises, especially on ecological resource protection roles. Today, shamanism survives primarily among indigenous peoples of the tundra, jungle, desert and other rural areas, and even in cities, towns, suburbs and shantytowns across northern Europe, Russia, Siberia, China, Japan, Korea, Indonesia, Australia, Africa, north, central and south America. This is especially true for Africa, and South America where Mestrzo shamanism is widespread.

The archaic role of the shaman can be found in the modern Chinese character 'Wu' meaning 'shaman'. It is made up of two characters, 'gong' or 'work' - the pillar symbol, and 'ren' or 'man, person' - that look like hands.

It is derived from an earlier Seal script character depicting, either someone in prayer or shaman dancing around a pillar or the long sleeves of a shaman. This glyph is thought to combine elements from two more archaic glyphs, one for 'dance' showing the long sleeved robes of a shaman and the oldest, the Cross Potent, symbolic of the quadrant of the Four Great Territories (Si Fang), representing the Wu Di, that is Di and the four Wu spirits of the directions. An archaic Da Chuan form of Shang dynasty oracle bone signs, shows a Cross Potent pictured with hands making offerings being received or given.

The rain rituals of female shamanism go back to prehistory. Some Shang oracle bone inscriptions show two shell glyphs over the character for 'woman' over the character for 'fire', indicating the Wu sat in the sun or surrounded by a ring of fire. This sacrificial act was a way of calling the rains. Showing a woman with shell decoration on her head, standing in fire, is explained as a kind of sympathetic magic that draws water by scorching a water element, in this case the female shaman as she sweats from exposure to heat.

'Wu' Standard script | hands praying or long sleeves | dancing around a pillar | Wu Di Cross Potent (Quadrant) | offerings recieved or given

shells, woman, fire | woman standing over fire | woman in circle of fire

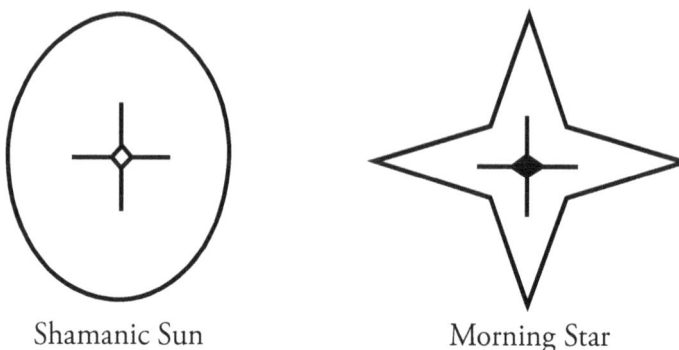

Shamanic Sun Morning Star

Shamanic Sun Symbol

The symbol of the shaman is often associated with the shamanic Sun symbol and the similarity between the Sun symbol and Morning Star symbol are evident. The Morning Star symbol was closely associated with the Native American Ghost Dance and adopted by famous Shaman like Sitting Bull. The Morning Star signifies the renewal tradition and resurrection of the past. It is a sign of courage and purity of spirit

Heartline

The Heartline represents the life force of an animal. When it reaches from the head to the heart of a bear, it symbolizes a warrior having the heart as strong as a bear.

Dream Catcher

First made by the Ojibwas tribe, a Dream Catcher is a handmade willow hoop woven into a web or net. They can include feathers or beads and are traditionally suspended on cradles as a form of love or protection. Dream catchers are widely viewed as a symbol of oneness and of Native American identity, widely accepted by the Pan Indian movement of the 1960s and 70s. However, Native Americans believe Dream Catchers have been appropriated by non-Native Americans. They can be found in virtually every New Age retail outlet in the West.

Medicine Wheel

Also known as the Sacred Hoop, the Medicine Wheel has been used by Native Americans for healing, protection and good health. It has four directions in a circle that represent the four element, the four seasons, stages of life, aspects of life, animals and plants. The symbol also represents the sky, earth and tree, that stand for health, life and rejuvenation.

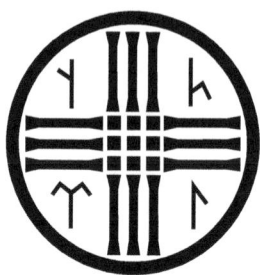

Tengri

Tengrism is the name given to Mongolian shamanism that has been influenced by Buddhism. It revolves around the worship of the Tengri or Ancestor Spirits and is devoted to Father Sky otherwise known as Tenger. Gengis Khan is considered one or the main embodiment of Tenger spirit.

Mongolian shamanic drums were made of horse skin. The drum standing for the saddle on which the shaman rode or the mount that carries the invoked spirit to the shaman. A symbol that appears on Tengi drums is a popular Tengri symbol featuring a 'shangrak', an equilateral cross in a circle, depicting the roof opening of a Yurt or tent. In its quadrants are the letters that spell put the name Tengri in Old Turkic runic script

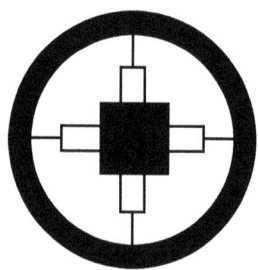

Dame Dame

An Adrinka symbol from Ghana, Africa, the Dame Dame is a representation of a traditional board game that carries the medicine of a sharp mind and keen perception. It helps one's mind find its 'focus', so that one can divert it into positive pathways and can beat the situations that surround us.

Daejong　　　　　　　　Sarn Daeguek

Daejongism

Daejongism or Great Ancestral Religion is a major form of Korean shamanism and the Daejong is its symbol. They worship Dagun or Tagun, one God manifest as a trinity of persons. In Daejongism, the Sarn Teaguk is the divine trinity. The swirling colours in the spherical symbol include yellow for humanity, red for the earth and blue for the heaven. All these three effect one another and need to be kept in balance.

Body Painting

Across all traditions, body and face painting are an important part of shamanic ritual. Paint is produced from minerals and berries and all participants in the ritual will be naked, wearing only body paint.

Traditional Shaman   Cernunos   Neoshaman

Antlered God (Cernunos)

Shamanism grew out of the Stone Age reindeer culture developed in Siberia by those hunting wild reindeer or those who maintained domesticated deer. The hunter in the deer skin 'transforms' from the world of people to the animal world, as he took on an independent power of the animal world. He became a mediator between worlds.

During the hunting magic ceremony, the hunter put on a deer skin and antlers and imitated deer behavior. They prayed for success using their bow and arrows as an accompaniment in these rituals, in which the bow and the antlers became symbols of their magic power.

A totemic ancestor came to the peoples world in the figure of a man, whilst shamans entered the ancestors world in the guise of a deer. These are the probable prototypes of an antlered deity that appeared during the Bronze age and developed during the Iron age as Cernunos.

The wearing of animal skins for ritual practises is called 'Skin Walking' by native Americans. It is a concept in which the shaman takes on an animal form such as a bear by wearing its skin or hide. One type of spirit that shaman attempt to contact are animal tutelary spirits called 'power animals' in Core Shamanism.

Male   Female

Mushroom Shaman (Santa Claus)

The taking of hallucinogenic mushrooms to commune with the spirit world, has been a part of shamanic ritual for millennia. Drawings of shaman symbolized by their mushroom shaped heads have been found in cave art from the Neolithic period onwards.

It is now thought that Santa Claus is a modern version of the mushroom shaman. The mushroom is the red and white Amanita Muscaria, more commonly known as the Fly Agaric mushroom that grows under conifers and birch trees across the northern hemisphere. Santa's red and white costume symbolizes he is a mushroom shaman.

In Siberia and the Arctic region, shaman dried out the Amanita mushrooms by hanging them on pine trees. To celebrate the Winter Solstice, shaman often dropped into people's houses with bags full of dried Amanita mushrooms as presents. This is why red and white baubles are hung from Xmas trees, it is why presents are wrapped in red and white paper and left under the Xmas tree during late December.

Santa's flying reindeer are symbolic of the shamans spirit journey. Rudolph's red nose symbolizes the Amanita mushroom as it lights the way ahead. Elves are the spirits that aid Santa in his journey. And, why else would Santa live at the North Pole ?

Shamanic Drum

Historically, drums figure heavily in the ritualistic activities of man. The beat of the drum attracts attention and invites some kind of physical response. The drum helps the shaman to travel in and out of the spirit world, used to enter an ecstatic state as well as a map the shaman used for orientation in the other realm.

With the virtual eradication of Shamanism in Europe it has become difficult to know the meaning of the symbols on the drum. Segmented drum patterns divide the drum surface, representing compass points or different levels of other worlds, forming geometric or abstract patterns, in which pictorial symbols representing stars, planets, spirits, men, animals and objects are placed.

Modern research introduces the idea that the drum skins are star maps featuring the Zodiac and separate constellations for the placement of symbols on the drum. It seems as though Christian symbols were incorporated into the nature religion of the shaman in a similar manner to the Icelandic runes called Galdrastafir.

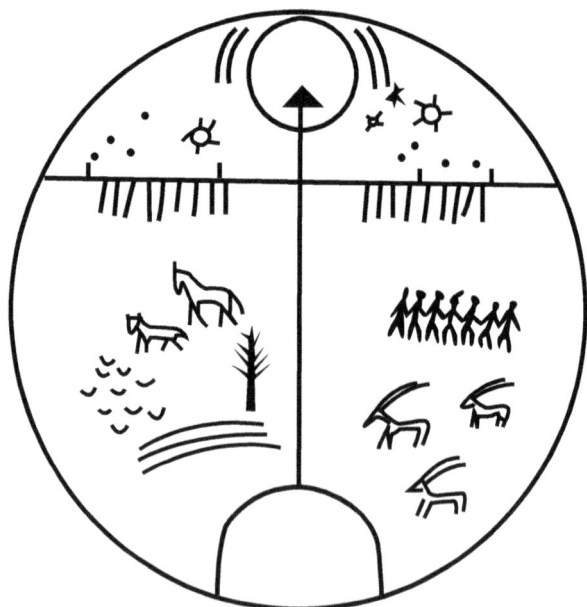

Traditional Siberian drum featuring the Shaman

PAGAN SIGILS

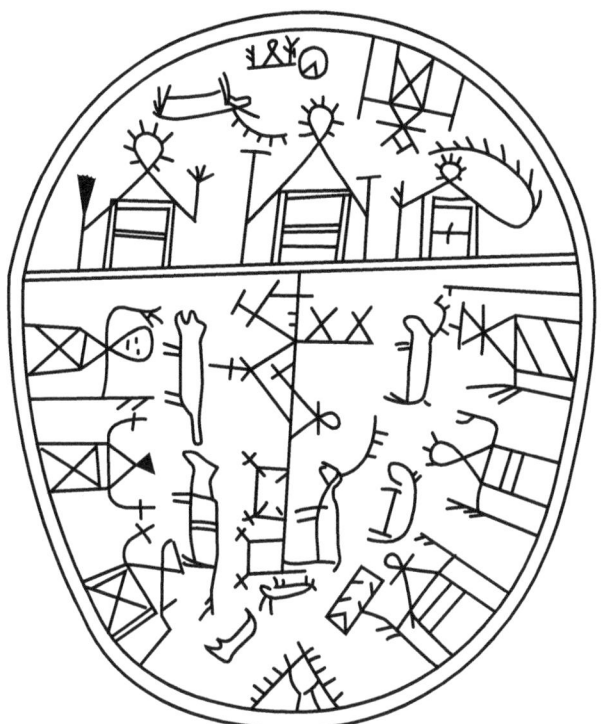

Traditional Sami drum

Contemporary Sami Drum

Healing Symbols

The use of symbols in healing rituals and meditation for a healthy mind, body and soul were used by ancient practises and continue to be used today. Healing symbols are said to be an effective way to obtain positive energy and rejuvenate the spirit.

The spiral sun symbolizes the shamans healing powers. The healer's hand symbol depicts the palm of one's hand with an open spiral originating from the center of the palm and running towards the fingers. The direction in which the spiral runs depends on the hand depicted, such as it opens between the index finger and thumb. The spiral is thought to symbolize the sun as the source of and energy.

The healing hand holds significance among the Hopi tribe. It is thought to represent 'hand to hand' combat, a loose translation could mean 'expert'. A possible explanation for the healing hand was reserved for shaman who had some form of healing and spiritual knowledge.

Turtles can live up to 150 years, which is why they symbolizes good health and a long life. The shell represents perseverance and protection. They are great embodiments of the earth, life force and our connection to the ancestors. The turtle is the great navigator that always finds its way home. As a symbol it conveys the medicine of the turtle with its closeness to home, security and safety. Turtle medicine comes with all that we need to live, which is the essence of prosperity.

Toads have been used in shamanic rituals going back hundreds of years. It is considered an healing animal and has a lot of spiritual and mystical importance as a representation of water, purification, fluidity, transparency and life itself.

Like frogs, toads are symbols of fertility because of their spawn. Because of their metamorphosis from tadpole to amphibian, the toad also represents transformation, rebirth, resurrection, a symbol of the power of change and adaptability that helps deal with adverse situations. Some toads also secrete toxins of various kinds that are used in traditional medicine that induce hallucinations, trances, comas and even death.

Spiral Sun

Healing Hand

Turtle　　　　　　　　Toad

New Age Movement

According to academics, the New Age has existed in many forms since the 2nd century CE. Beginning with Gnosticism, New Age ideas have continued through a variety of groups including the Rosicrucians, Freemasons and Theosophists.

The establishment of Spiritualism in the USA during the 1840s has been identified as a precursor to the New Age. Further influences on the New Age include the American escotericist Edgar Cayce, Danish mystic Mortinus and psychologist Carl Jung.

Some academics also say that the direct descendents of the New Age can be found in the UFO religions of the 1950s, with strong apocalyptic beliefs regarding a coming new age, which would be brought about by contact with extraterrestrials.

The New Age movement has its roots in Theosophy with its synthesis of the notion of evolutionary progress with chiefly Hindu-Buddhist religious concepts. The early New Age movement was based largely in Britain and is most associated with the Counter Culture of the 1960s.

The Beatles adoption of Hinduism and their study of Transcendental Meditation kick started the Human Potential movement that subsequently became the New Age. Also found within 60s Counter Culture is the use of the terms 'New Age' and 'Age of Aquarius' used in reference to the coming era.

The decade also saw a variety of new religious movements. In Britain, a number of small groups that came to be identified as the 'light' movement had begun declaring the existence of a coming New Age. In the USA, many were just variations on Hinduism, Buddhism and Sufism, including the San Francisco Zen Center, the Inner Peace movement and the Church of Satan. All of these groups created the spiritual milieu from which the New Age emerged, representing a synthesis of many previous movements and strands of thought and imagery.

At the end of the 1960s, many former members of the Counter Culture became early adherents of the New Age movement that emerged throughout the 70s and entered its full development in the early 1980s. By the late 80s, publishers had stopped using the term New Age as a marketing device using Mind, Body, Spirit, instead. The New Age attitude of spiritual individualism and eclecticism influenced the development of British Rave culture in the late 1980s and 1990s.

New Age spiritual ideas and practises are adopted from other, particularly non-western cultures including Hindu/Buddhists philosophies such has Tantra, Yoga and Vedanta, Chinese practises like Feng Shui, Qi Giong and Tai Chi, Native American spiritual medicine, and Australian Aboriginal dream working.

Neopaganism and the New Age are often confused because of significant overlap between the two religious movements. They can be described as different streams of occult culture that overlap at points. Many pagans distance themselves from the New Age movement, even using the term as an insult within their communities. New Ager's criticize pagans for valuing the material world over the spiritual.

The New Age movement is accused of cultural imperialism, misappropriating sacred ceremonies, exploitation of the intellectual and cultural property of indigenous peoples and of appropriating a lot of spiritual symbols from across the globe from different cultures, generating a lot of criticism from established Christian organizations as well as Neopagans and indigenous communities. Neopagans have also been accused of cultural appropriation.

Native American spiritual leaders have denounced the New Age misappropriation of their sacred ceremonies and other intellectual property, saying that the value of these instructions and ceremonies when led by unauthorized people are questionable, maybe meaningless and harmful to the individual carrying false messages.

They reject the expropriation of their ceremonial ways by non-Indians. They see the New Age movement as either not fully understanding, deliberately trivializing or distorting their way of life and have declared war on all such plastic medicine people, the white man's shaman who have no genuine connection to the traditions they claim to represent.

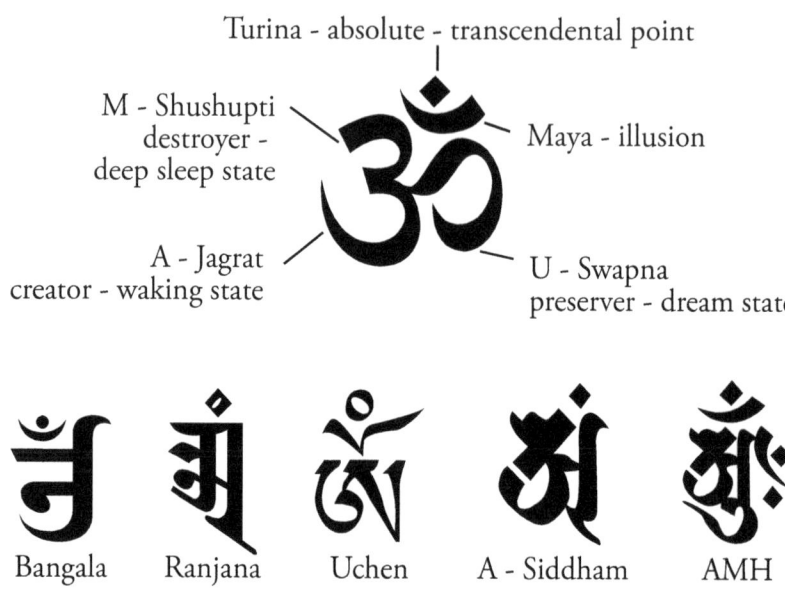

OM / AUM (Akaram Ukaram Makaram)

OM is the universal name of the Divine and has different spellings such as AUM and AHM. It was first mentioned in the mystical texts of the Upanishads, associated with Vedanta or Vedic philosophy. OM is not a word but rather an intonation which, like music, transcends the barriers of age, race and culture. It is made up of three Sanskrit letters, A U M, when combined together they make the sound AUM or OM. It is believed to be the basic sound of the world and to contain all other sounds.

OM is the highest faculty of consciousness. 'A' as the waking consciousness or Jagrat.' U' is the dream consciousness or Svapna and 'M' as the consciousness during deep sleep or Susupti. OM as a whole represents the all encompassing cosmic consciousness or Turiya, on the fourth plane, beyond words and concepts, the consciousness of the fourth dimension.

The symbolic meaning of OM is the same no matter which calligraphic variant OM is written in. Tantric Buddhism employs the independent vowel 'A' sign to represent OM. Thus, OM is used to signify divinity and authority and is akin to the word 'Amen.'

Sri Yantra

Yantra is a Sanskrit word meaning 'instrument'. They are geometrical designs which can represent a deity or divine figure, making the process of evolution conscious to the adept of Tantra. All primal shades of a yantra are psychological symbols corresponding to inner states of human consciousness. The sacred symbols of the process of involution and evolution.

Generally made of several concentric figures (squares, circles, lotuses, triangles, point). The point (bindu) at the center of the yantra signifies unity, the origin, the principle of manifestation and emanation. When these concentric figures are gradually growing away from its center (bindu) in stages, this is a symbol of the process of macrocosmic evolution. When they are gradually growing towards its center, this is a symbol of the process of microcosmic evolution.

Somaya Maha Dharma

Mandala

Mandala meaning 'circle' in Sanskrit, is a sacred, symbolic diagram, a visual aid to attain desirable mental states. A mandala can be defined in two ways, as a schematic representation of the universe or, internally as a guide for several psychological practises that take place in many Asian traditions, including meditation.

In Tantric Buddhism, there are four types of mandala. The Maha Mandalas depict the Buddhas and Bodhisattvas in human form. Somaya Mandalas show them as objects. Dharma Mandalas show them as bija. Karma Mandalas are three dimensional sculptural mandalas like Angkor Wat.

Dharma mandalas with only bija are regarded as the most sublime, the vision of one who is totally awake. Outside of India, the esoteric practises related to Sanskrit script, especially the writing and recitation of mantra, remained widespread but in general there was a simplification of the incredibly complex Indian tantric doctrines in China and Japan. Emphasis was placed on seed syllables especially in conjunction with mandalas.

In China, the sound mattered less than its written form. In fact, nothing in China had any real value unless put in writing. Chinese and Japanese Buddhist monks created large, complex mandalas that viewed the cosmos in the form of Buddhas represented as bijaksara.

Lantsa (Ranjana)

Vartu (cursive Ranjana)

Mantra (Om Mani Padme Hum)

Mantra is an organic language in which sound and meaning correspond as sound-ideas. The spiritual expression of sound is found in poetry and music, which are synthesized in the one profound and all embracing vibration of the sacred syllable or bija-mantra. In Tantra, everything in Creation is formed from air that resonates as sound. This sound is called the "Word". This is not ordinary words or Sabda of which speech is composed, it is Mantra or "instruments of thought" which create a mental picture with its sound.

In India, not only the Word but every sound of which it consists, every letter of the alphabet, is looked upon as a sacred symbol. The letters of the alphabet are mantras or sacred prayer syllables, linking the practitioner to a particular divine principle. Each letter is charged with energy that creates vibrations in the inner consciousness of the devotee. Mantra are tools for thinking and worshipping. Meditating on mantra, shapes the mind and makes it pure.

Om Mani Padme Hum is probably the most famous Tantric mantra, particularity associated with Tibetan Buddhism. The mantra of the Boddhisattva called Avalokkitesvara, the Mahavaircana, the compassionate aspect of Buddha. It is written from right to left in any of four scripts styles.

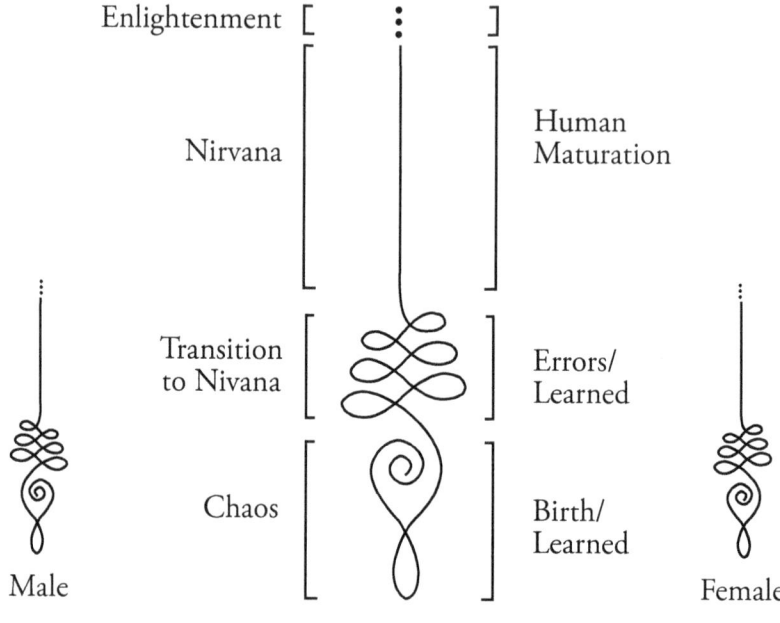

Umalome

Sak Yant is a form of tattoo art that originated in Thailand and to a lesser extent in Cambodia, Laos and Myanmar. Its popularity among the masses, fueled by western celebrity endorsement, have turned many modern day Thai's to view Sak Yant symbolism as nothing more than stylish amulets and talismans or good luck charms, so much so that some are asking for a complete ban of any tattoo of religious figures like Buddha.

The spiral designs called Umalome indicate the earthly distractions we encounter in our daily lives. As we grow older and wiser, this spiral gradually decreases until it becomes a straight line pointing downwards. This signifies the path to Nirvana or true enlightenment.

There are many variations but the overall shape remains the same. It starts with a spiral at one end and then slowly unfurls into a series of twists and turns, eventually the line straightens out. In some versions the lines is completed with a single dot. All these components symbolize the various shapes we encounter in our spiritual journey's.

Cho Ku Rei

Sei He Ki

Hon Sho Sha Nen

Dai Ko Myo

Raku

Reiki Symbols

Reiki symbols are the healing symbols which manifest the flow of universal life energy or Reiki. They act as keys that open the doors towards a higher level of awareness, consciousness, awakening and enlightenment. Based on the Japanese writing system called Kanji, their origin is said to be from Sanskrit, the ancient language of the Hindu Vedas. There is no right way to draw a Reiki symbol, the symbols of every master are drawn differently and all the ways are right.

There are five major Reiki symbols, the power symbol Cho Ku Rei is used to increase or decrease power. The mental or emotional symbol Sei He Ki symbolizes harmony, its intention is purification. The distance symbol Han Sha Ze Sho is used when sending Qi across long distances. The master symbol Dai Ko Myo represents all that is Reiki. Its intention is enlightenment. The completion symbol Raku is used during the final stage of Reiki attunment. Its intention is grounding.

Double Happiness

The character for Double Happiness is an archaic good luck symbol used by practitioners of Feng Shui. This piece of Chinese calligraphy is a decorative symbol of Love and pervades its bliss into a marriage. It is formed of two Chinese characters for 'satisfaction' or 'Xi'.

Shou

The Chinese symbol for 'long life'. The symbols mainly demonstrates the five pillars of philosophy, responsibility, nobility, awareness, strength and wisdom. It is found on jewelry, textiles, furniture, architecture and on a wedding gift to give well wishes to the newly married couple.

PAGAN SIGILS

Fu Xi - snake   ancient - fish   modern - fish

Taijitu Tushuo   Zhou Huigian   Lai Zhide
11th c.   14th c.   16th c.

Taijitu / Tai Chi Tu

Known as the Yin/Yang symbol in the West, in the East it is known as the Tai Chi symbol. The I Ching refers to it as the "Taijitu" or "Diagram of the Supreme Ultimate". The original written Chinese character for 'I Ching' is a compound character combining the words 'Sun' on top, and 'Moon' on the bottom.

After observing the Universe from the sun/moon philosophy, they found that the universe changes everyday, it has seasonal and annual cycles, from these cycles the unchanging rules are created.

The principle of Yin Yang is represented in Daoism by the icon called Taijitu. In modern Chinese, it is commonly used to mean the simple 'divided circle' form (tai chi/harmony), but it may refer to any of the several schematic diagrams that contain at least one circle with an inner pattern of symmetry representing yin and yang.

There is one basic form with several variants, conceived around the idea of two interlocking spirals, commonly described as two snakes or two fishes, resting head to tail against each other with each spiral featuring an inverse dot.

There is no official standardized rendition, but various portrayals have appeared through the millennia, with many 'artistic' variations created in the 20th and 21st century, as exemplified by western tattoo artists.

Pa Kua / Bagau

This ancient Chinese system of philosophical divination dates back to at least the 8th century BC and is still in use today. Called Bagau in the West, Pa Kua is a Chinese term meaning 'eight symbols'. It is used to describe the Daoist religious motif that incorporates the octagonal arrangement of the 8 trigrams of the I Ching, sometimes arranged around the symbol called Taijitu, denoting the balance of yin and yang.

In the I Ching, Heaven or positive yang is symbolized by an unbroken line and Earth or negative yin is symbolized by a broken line. A trigram is made up of three of these lines to form the eight combinations of yin and yang. These eight trigrams or Pa Kua are then paired with themselves and every other trigram to produce the 64 hexagrams of the I Ching. These simple yet profound symbols encompass the universal source of all things, known as the Dao.

The eight trigrams arranged in the Bagau motif are conceptually a template or ruler within Daoist cosmology to track change. There are two types of Bagau, firstly the Xiantian used in exorcism. It also features in the Chinese martial arts styles of Bagauzhang and Ying Ji Quan. Secondly, the Houtain used for divination. In Feng Shui, the Houtain is regarded as the pattern of determining the significance and auspicious qualities of special relationships.

Xiantian or Xiantiantu translates as Precelestial, Primordial, Prenatal, Early Heaven or Before Heaven. It is also called the Fu Xi sequence, after the legendary Emperor Fu Xi, who was inspired by a pattern on the back of a mythical Dragon Horse, to create the eight trigrams and arrange them in the octagonal motif known as the Precelestial Pa Kua.

Houtain or Houtaintu translates as Postcelestial, Posterior, Postnatal, After Heaven or Later Heaven. It is also called the Manifest Bagau and the King Wen sequence. Chinese legend tells that King Wen 1152-1056 BCE, was inspired to change the order of the Fu Xi bagau, by the pattern on the shell of a mythical Dragon Turtle. The number of dots on its shell formed a 3 x 3 magic square known as the Luoshu.

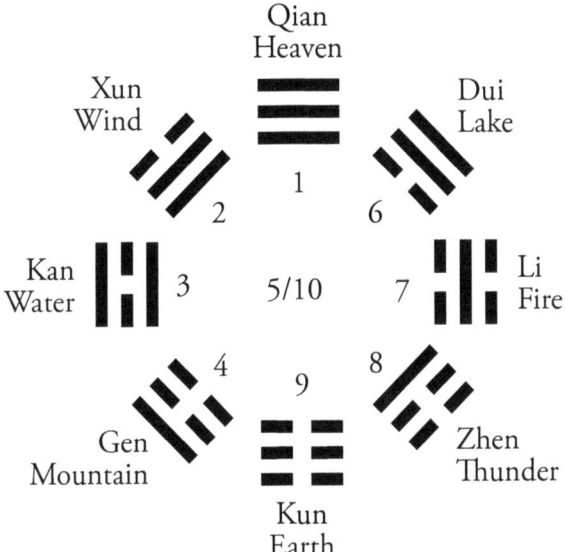

Fu Xi / Xiantian - Pre-celestial sequence

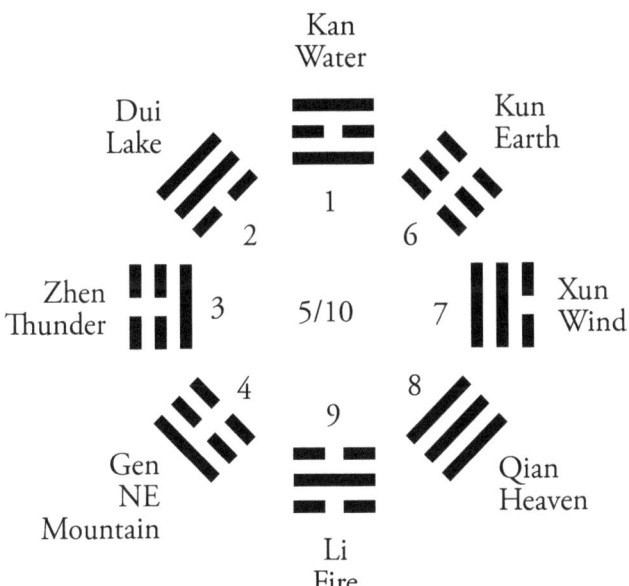

King Wen / Houtian - Post-celestial sequence

New Age Spirituality

New Age spirituality promotes the development of the persons own power or divinity. The New Age believes we ourselves are God. When referring to deity, a follower of this type of spirituality is not talking about a transcendental, personal God who created the Universe, but is referring to a higher consciousness within themselves. A person pursuing spiritual development would see themselves as deity, the cosmos, the universe. In fact, everything that the person sees, hears, feels or imagines is considered divine.

Highly eclectic, New Age spirituality is a collection of ancient spiritual traditions, taught by a vast array of speakers, books and seminars. It acknowledges Gods and Goddesses as in Hinduism. The Earth is viewed as the source of all spirituality, it has an intelligence, emotions and deity. But superseding all is Self. Self is the originator, controller and power over all. There is no reality outside of what the person determines.

The Lucis Trust symbol is a New Age symbol used in meditation and symbolizes a number of interrelated energies with which to bring into being the new paradigm of the Aquarian age.

The outer blue circle represents the second ray field of solar logic and contains the cosmic cross of Sirius. The background is the golden disc representing the Will of God or Shambala. The Yellow Triangle represents the spiritual hierarchy of Ascended Masters, Bhuddi or Love. The Blue Star or blue pentagram represents the highest level of consciousness humanity as a unit can embody at this time. The small White Cross in the center represents the equal armed cross of future Aquarian activity.

Humanist Movement

Designed by Dennis Barrington, the Happy Human won a competition in 1965 to become the symbol of the British Humanist Association. First known as the Happy Man, the symbol has been tailored for individual organizations such as the International and Gay and Lesbian Humanist Associations.

Eckankar

The Eckankar church of Minnesota USA is a modern religion founded in 1965. It is not affiliated with any other religious group. Followers believe its purpose is to help individuals find their way back to God through direct personal, spiritual experiences.

The movement teaches simple spiritual exercises, such as singing 'Hu' called a 'love song to God', to experience the Light and Sound of God and recognize the Holy Spirit. The final spiritual goal of all Eckists is to become conscious 'coworkers' with God.

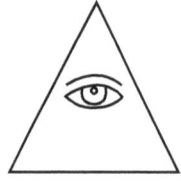 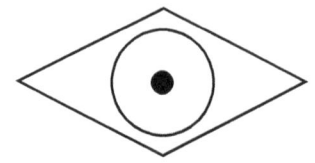 

All Seeing Eye

The All Seeing Eye is a symbol of divine omniscience. It symbolizes a persons own inner divine spark and spiritual insight. It is connected with the sitting meditation position, the body forming a pyramid with the eyes in the eye position, reaching a state of single-eyed-ness in meditation.

Over time, the symbol has been corrupted and co-opted from a benevolent symbol of the higher power watching over us, into its opposite representing an evil power, a controlling elite of 1%, separated from the humanity at the top of the pyramid. Since it first appeared in US Freemasonry, it has symbolized control and domination of a shady elite called the Illuminati.

Ruchu - original   alternative

Raelian Star

The Raelians are a US UFO religious cult founded in the 1960s. They believe that planet Earth was created by a people who came from the sky but not from God. These sky people are extraterrestrials called the Elohim in Hebrew and the Anunaki is ancient Sumerian. Their symbol was compromised of a six pointed star or hexagram whose arms cleverly morphed into the ancient sun symbol, the swastika. After its adoption, the swastika was removed 'lest it might cause offence' and replaced by a spiral variant resembling a spinning galaxy.

Peace Sign

This modern spiritual symbol signifies wholeness, as a blessing to 'live well'. Its origins lie in the 1958 British Campaign for Nuclear Disarmament. From there it quickly became a universal sign for peace and appropriated by both the 1960s Counter Culture and the New Age movement in the 1980s.

   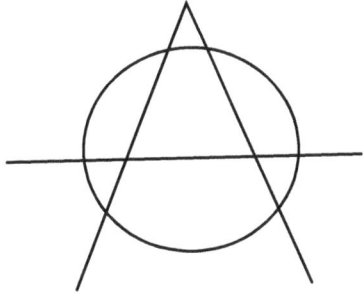

Modern   Post Modern

Anarchy symbol

Originally a capital A contained within a circle of the same thickness of line. The post-modern version was inspired by the anarcho-punk band Crass, who saw it graffitied on a wall in France and adopted it The lines represent a breaking out of the circle. Since the 1980s it has been used by many New Age adherents to express their socio-political attitude towards mainstream society.

One World Religion

As opposed to the 'Apocalyptic' nature of Christianity, the New Age has a generally more optimistic view of humankind's future. Believing in the transition into the Age of Aquarius or the New Age. A spiritual transformation that will bring about a new dawning of oneness of the human family.

As such New Age beliefs seep into popular consciousness, the movements original attempt to reconcile the realm of religion and science that enhances the human condition, both spiritually and materially, has led to an eclectic embracing of almost every religious icon and mystical symbol made by man since the beginning of time. Accepting the ageless wisdom of the world's great religious traditions. Allocating them all equal status in the pantheon of world faiths, as a part of its holistic view of faith.

Further Reading

Hermetica, Hermes Trismegistus, 1st/4th c. CE, Egyptian

Keys of Solomon, 14th/15th c. Italian

Malleus Maleficourus, Heinrich Krammer, 1486, German

Lesser Keys of Solomon, 16th/17th c., Italian

Eddas, 16th/17th c, Iceland

Galdrabok, 16th/17th c. Iceland

Grimoirium Verum, Albeck the Egyptian, 18th c. Italian

Isis Unveiled, Helena Blavatsky 1877

Secret Doctrine, Helena Blavatsky 1888

Book of Ceremonial Magic, Arthur Edward White 1896

Gospel of the Witches, Charles Godfrey Leland 1899

Book of Law, Aleiser Crowely 1904

Holy Book of Thelema, Aleister Crowley, 1909

Magic in Theory and Practise, Aleister Crowely 1929

The White Goddess, Robert Graves, 1945

Book of Shadows, Gerald Gardner 1952

Witchcraft Today, Gerald Gardner 1954

The Satanic Bible, Anton Le Vey, 1969

The Way of the Shaman, Michael Harner, 1980

Holy Book of Women's Mysteries, Zsunnanna Bucharest, 1986

The Alchemist, Paulo Coelho, 1988

The New Earth, Eckhart Tolle, 2005

Element Encyclopedia of Secret Symbols, Adele Norden, Harper Element 2008

Web

encyclopedia.com

learnreligion.com

worldhistory.org

broadshawfoundation.php

novoscriptorium.com

theworldmayknow.com

symbolikon.com

symboldictionary.com

ancient-symbols.com

sacredtexts.com

theoi.com

taoistiching.org

wiccaacademy.com

galdrasrafir.com

historiska.com

thuleia.com

gaia.com

shamanlinks.net

theosophicalsociety.org.uk

thelemicorder.io

ideas.ted.com (ice age symbols)

da.style (Slavic symbols)

vk.com (Irminism/Odindism)

latvians.com (runes)

gutenberg.com (pagan and christian symbols)

wordpress.com (cult of the mother goddess)

www.ingramcontent.com/pod-product-compliance
Ingram Content Group UK Ltd.
Pitfield, Milton Keynes, MK11 3LW, UK
UKHW021516061225
465807UK00005BA/32